IN THE BACKYARDS OF OUR LIVES

AND OTHER ESSAYS

RUSHWORTH KIDDER

IN THE BACKYARDS OF OUR LIVES

AND OTHER ESSAYS

YANKEE BOOKS

Printed in the United States of America

Book designer: Ann Aspell
Cover designer: Ann Aspell
Book packager: Nan K. Smith

ISBN 0–89909–343–4 hardcover

Distributed in the book trade by St. Martin's Press

2   4   6   8   10   9   7   5   3   hardcover

CONTENTS

□

PREFACE

□

The other day, as I was pulling these essays together, I took the dog up into the woods beyond the stream. We climbed up to the gap in the old stone wall that opens onto Orville Young's high field. Orville used to captain one of the schooners that still makes summer tourist runs out into Penobscot Bay, and, if he didn't invent the word "ship-shape," he should have. Everything he puts his hand to neatens right up: his house, his shingled barn, his cars, his lawn. When he cut a stand of pine near the road a while back, he fixed up a lot of birdhouses on sticks and nailed them to the stumps, all straight and true and prim-looking. "Orville's bird-condos," my daughters promptly christened them.

He keeps his high field that way, too, even though it goes for months on end without anyone seeing it. Every summer he puts his sickle-bar on the tractor and cuts it meticulously, rakes and bales the hay, and cleans up behind. There's not a rock or stump anywhere in sight.

Looking out from that field, you see nothing but woods between you and the back of Mount Megunticook a couple of miles off. In all that panorama, there's not a dwelling in sight except Orville's old Cape. There's hardly an open field, either: just the tops of trees, blending into a carpet that runs up the mountain and down the other side into the sea.

That's not how it's always looked. This area was once a patchwork of fields—and not so many years ago, either. The recent history of New England is a tale of overgrowth, seedlings of white pine and gray birch taking hold around the edges of pastures and creeping toward the center. Let a hayfield go without mowing for a few seasons, and the saplings are too big for the sickle bar. In another ten years, you've got a stand of tent poles, and in twenty, a pretty good woodlot.

But if nature easily claims back the fields, it's not so good at erasing the boundaries. You can't usually walk more than a couple of hundred yards through the woods around here before you come upon an old stone wall. You can tell when you're approaching one, too. When you spot a pine or maple three feet across, you can be pretty sure it marks a fence line. No one would have let a tree stand in the middle of a field long enough to get that size. The walls themselves are all a-tumble, of course. Frost is the great leveler in New England, in more ways than this one. But the stones are still there, where the first farmers put them when they cleared the pastures. In the late fall, when the ground was dry but the snow hadn't come, they'd go out and rebuild the walls. You could let a wall go longer than a pasture without attention, but not much. Sooner or later a winged maple seed would find its way into the earth below the rocks and push a tree right up through, and you'd have to go at it with an ax and a grubbing hoe if you wanted to keep the wall in the same place.

I've always liked those walls. Even back in the forgotten woodlots, they provide a kind of definition. In that, they remind me of that other great New England tradition, writing. I think of this part of the world as a place of words. Partly, I suppose, that's because our forefathers took to the Bible the way their descendants take to self-help books—to find out how to live better—and they made sure their children could read well enough to do the same. Add to that the long winter, dark by mid-afternoon and bitter cold, and the idea of huddling indoors around the fire with a few candles and a book looks pretty attractive.

I don't pretend these essays were all written in front of a fire by candlelight, though I can think of a few that were. But I guess that as a native New Englander who has lived in every one of these six states but Vermont, I've taken on some of those old verbal habits almost without knowing it. Like the stone walls, these essays are efforts at definition—a setting of boundaries, a way to put edges on the vast patchwork of experience. I suppose I write them for the same reason Orville hays his fields and the old boys tended their walls. Because if you don't, the lushness of life grows up faster than you can come to terms with it, and pretty soon the whole thing is all saplings and woodchucks.

Besides, I like personal essays for pretty much the same reason I like walking in the woods. You don't do it to get somewhere, but for the sake of the walk itself. It

slows you down and forces you to notice little things—
the rusted blade of a crosscut saw, the deer print in
the mud, the mound of pine-cone bits left by a squirrel
on a mossy stump. It makes you look hard at your own
backyard.

If these essays have anything in common beyond the
obvious subject matter of a New Englander trying to come
to terms with a part of the world that's less a place than a
habit of mind, I suppose it's a question of feelings. I've
spent a lot of time as a journalist writing about facts and
events, where objectivity is the goal. But I've never quite
been comfortable merely describing exteriors. I always
want to get at what's going on underneath. Essays are the
place to do that. These essays are also about the way
words work, not simply to describe but to create experience. Wallace Stevens, another New Englander, once
noted that "Poetry is the subject of the poem." Language,
similarly, is the subject of the essay. That's especially true
for essays about New England, which is not so much a
place seen as a way of seeing.

A note on locations: Many of these pieces describe
my upbringing in Amherst, Massachusetts. A few center
on an old farmhouse my wife and I helped restore in
Cornish Flat, New Hampshire, or on a summer home my
family had in Canada—which in many ways is New
England under a different flag. And, of course, a lot of
them touch on Maine, where we now live. Most of them
were first published on The Home Forum pages of *The
Christian Science Monitor.*

Lincolnville, Maine
August 1991

IN TOUCH
WITH
THE WORLD

☐

His name was George Bean, and he advertised himself as the Yankee Auctioneer. By the time I was ten, he was at the height of his powers; and whenever his big boxy vans came to town, and his tent mushroomed up overnight on a patch of lawn near some recently sold house, he drew folks from several states around. I came, too; and though he never knew it, he spoke a single word one July morning that rearranged my sense of the world beyond western Massachusetts.

Mr. Bean was an auctioneer of the old school. Words were his real stock in trade. Filled with patter and jokes, he was also possessed of a turn of phrase that made you want to sell your wagon, trade away all your marbles, and barter your jackknife to buy the drabbest objects. He had a wry wit, too, and knew just when the audience needed to be told that some ugly lump of junk was, in fact, an ugly lump of junk.

He was at his best, however, when the actual bidding began. He would open up with a singsong torrent of words so run together and so headlong that you felt you had to bid just to give him a chance to catch his breath. Maybe he never had to breathe; or maybe he could suck in air while he was talking. Whatever his secret, he was a marvel to hear: "Startingatfive, who'llsay fivefivefive doIhearafive Thank You, five, now sevengimmmesevenseven whatamIbid THERE'S seven now ten, where's ten thankyoudownfront twelvetwelvetwelve needanice crisp clean twelve-dollar-bill whose got twelve AND fif-teen, fif-teen goin' at fif-teen. . . . " He was tireless, he was flawless. He was the great American evangelist of Yankee bargain-hunting, converting us all from his tent-covered pulpit with the brimstone of his secular preaching. The numbers rose and fell, the objects came and went, and still the voice surged onward.

The audience, of course, had neither his stamina nor his persistence. Pulled three ways at once by the sound of his voice, the fascination of the goods set about for inspection on the lawn, and the lure of the ladies selling doughnuts at the back, we wandered in and out of the tent among the rows of folding wooden chairs. And as we prowled, the inventory dwindled. Elegant highboys were knocked down to prosperous-looking strangers for prices quite beyond comprehension. Overwrought vases and dangerous-looking chandeliers disappeared into the backs of the station wagons of local matrons. But the most exciting things—the crate of handleless ax heads and rusted hunting knives, the two-seater bicycle wanting only pedals and chain and one seat, the home-built riding lawn mower solemnly promised to need only a new spark plug—were the preserve of boys, their dads, and ordinary folk. There was always the hope that the bike would be held off until later, when the tent was nearly empty. Would it, could it, go for only two dollars? But the bidding always seemed to creep upward toward princely sums like eight-fifty, which none of us boys could even begin to match. More than once, I recall, we went home with nothing to show for our waiting but the grease of a few doughnuts at the corners of our mouths.

But one July day—even as I write of it across a quarter-century's span I can feel again the pitch of my own eagerness and the expectation of disappointment—I had gone early, parked my bike in a bush, checked to see that my entire liquid assets (three dollars, I think) were safe in my pocket, and sidled up to the tent. And there, on the still-dewy grass, it stood: an old stand-up radio in a polished wooden case, nearly as tall as I was. It was almost unscratched. All its wooden knobs were in place, and even the gold grill-cloth over the massive speaker was unblemished. The dial—a wide glass strip set into a foot-long brass frame—spoke of untold wonders: four different long-wave and short-wave bands, with colored dots and tiny letters marking the famous stations, American and foreign.

It was enough to make a small boy burst. I could see at a glance that it must be beyond my reach. To be sure, it was not yet an antique: small-tubed radios had recently come in, and people were still busy replacing these older prewar models. But it was lovely, and I could see in the eyes of the men who were beginning to arrive that it would not be given away.

I bode my time, however, and pretty soon the auction started. I pretended an interest in the tasseled lamp-

shades and china cups that passed before me. At last Mr.
Bean got around to the radio. I was sitting right down in
front when his helpers—it took two of them—brought it
in. He didn't seem disposed to spend much time on its
merits. To him, I guess, it was just a warm-up for antiques
yet to come. So he tossed a few words at it, and then
asked, "What am I bid?"

I think I leaped from my chair. I'm sure I shot my
hand in the air. And I know I hollered as loudly as I could,
"One dollar!"

There must have been, in the heart of that canny
Yankee auctioneer, something of the spirit of Christmas
that July day. He looked hard at me for less time than it
takes to write this, and then his round features broke into
a grin. He picked up his gavel, tapped it on the block, and
said, "Sold!"

The tent erupted. "Hey, wait a minute!" I heard a man
shout from the back. "You can't do that!" said another
voice, as someone else yelled, "Five dollars!"

I sat quivering. But old Mr. Bean stood his ground. He
gaveled the crowd to silence. Then, in a voice full of both
severity and delight, he said, "I said sold, and I mean sold,
to the lad in the front for one doll-ah!"

What happened next I don't precisely recall. The
howls subsided, I guess, and I fumbled out a dollar for the
lady at the side desk, and probably called my mom to
come get me and my prize. I do remember a couple of
grudging congratulations from some disbelieving men.

And the radio? It worked like a dream. Many a night I
lay in bed listening to Rochester, New York, or Wheeling,
West Virginia, or Radio Moscow, or the BBC. As I said, old
Mr. Bean put me in touch with the world.

DECODINGS
IN THE
NIGHT

□

It was a splendid antenna. The black enamelled wire hung taut between huge spruces, riding high across the house. From the glass insulator in the middle a lead looped down to my brother's upstairs window, vanishing through a hole beneath the sill. Twilights, when the light was right, the insulator seemed to hover unsuspended, buoyed up by itself.

Behind the window my brother's small hand-built transmitter hummed and glowed: a black wrinkle-finished slab of steel, all set about with knobs and jacks and dials, wired in fifteen ways to other boxes and panels. And there, late into the nights, he sat between headphones and Morse code key, tapping out into the charged and mysterious night the blips and splashes of sound that stand for words. "CQ, CQ, CQ," said his key: the short-wave amateur's coded invitation to conversation with others. Bouncing over the Pelham Hills, blanketing the Berkshires, bounding down the Atlantic seaboard, the call went out in search of an answer. The map on his wall was forested with colored pins, clustered like forgotten candy around Massachusetts and standing proud and alone and important in far-off Cincinnati and Savannah—the notched gunstock of a hunter for words, the record of answers picked out across hundreds of miles and sifted from a rabble of unmeaning noises, alien and remote.

I was ten years his junior, and my world, not yet of signals and words, was still an outdoor one. Afternoons, when the weather was fine, I played about under the larger spruce or climbed up it as far as I dared. Laddering my way among the limbs, I marked out my own home-made map. Sap Drip was a mound of pitch gummed onto the butt of a limb twenty feet above the ground; Sap Bucket, a few branches beyond, was the gash oozing out the drops that made Sap Drip. Then came The Weights, a clanking and cumbersome bunch of sash-weights and small steel girders which, roped to the antenna through a pulley, counterweighted the wire and kept it tight as the trees moved in the wind. At last came The Pulley itself, where the antenna began its outbound funicular.

Up to that level, my vertical stack of hamlets was known and secure. Beyond, however, lay the frontier, an uncharted tower of narrowing trunk, thinning branches, and the ever-swaying wind. Some days, braver than others, I'd climb past The Pulley, above chimneys and lower trees and telephone lines, to the level of the weathercock on a neighboring steeple. There, looking down on the antenna and out to the woods and hills far away, I sent out my own imagined signals: CQ, CQ, CQ, the answering wind making wordy noises among the cones above my head.

It was on one such afternoon, I remember, that I composed my first poem. I was eight, and words, not yet either mystery or miracle, seemed to lie about in great uncultured hunks, ready to be broken off by any passerby and whittled leisurely into sense or nonsense, whichever seemed best. The poem was about late afternoon; and, as I now see, it wasn't particularly good. But so special was its feeling and the impact of its wholly unannounced coming that I still, decades away, remember it clearly. It contained the lines:

> I often take my sword and spear
> And play that I'm in atmosphere.

Atmosphere, I later learned, was not, as I had thought, another word for outer space. But I didn't have anything else handy to rhyme with *spear*—though why I needed a spear for space travel remains to this day a mystery. Logic notwithstanding, however, the poem was duly submitted to my third-grade teacher, a wonderful woman with the not entirely irrelevant name of Miss Powers. Somehow it got sent to the local paper, where it crackled into print. CQ, CQ, CQ, it tapped out. And friends and neighbors, responding with dutiful congratulations, found a small boy, quizzical and unsure, ambushed by a commitment to words that he never asked for and was pretty sure he didn't want.

But the air is full of signals powering out into the waiting snares of our antennae. The poems that get themselves written down—what are they but the signals that happen, as one spins the dial, to break out so clearly and loudly that the listener stops and listens and

7

decodes? Late into the night, thought teems with poetry: and you and I and every shaper of language, whether or not we put pencil to paper, are potentially the poet and reader to our own lives.

I think that's what Dylan Thomas must have seen—what both elated and worried him. His poems and stories are alive with recollections of his childhood in Wales, evocative and open-eyed wonderings about the goings-on of a world of parks and schoolyards and alleyways and gardens and, most of all, of words. One of his early poems ends, rather simply for him, on a note both sad and satisfying. "The ball I threw while playing in the park," he writes, "has not yet reached the ground."

So much hangs suspended—so much of childhood, of delight, of carefree exuberance—waiting to be garnered into poetry. So many unsent invitations to conversation with a reader; so many decodings in the night; so many listenings: CQ, CQ, CQ. . . .

IT DON'T HARDLY MATTER

☐

The braided cable, black with age, snaked down the side of our flat-roofed Victorian house, past the green shutters and corniced windows, and disappeared into the earth. I kept my tricycle well away from it. My father, who took me out on the roof to show me the lightning rods spiring upward from the looming brick chimneys, explained that the cable would send any lightning to strike harmlessly into the ground. There was no danger in touching it, he said, when there were no storms around. I wasn't so sure.

But he was patient in his explanations: He said the house had been built in what was, a century earlier, an open field. Like its neighbors, it had needed protection from the summer thunderstorms that charged across western Massachusetts. Since then, however, the spruces had towered above the house on every side, and the metal-tipped steeple of the Methodist church had risen impressively next door. I was comforted in knowing that

9

they, rather than our copper spikes, would probably draw off any nearby thunderbolts. Still, those rods seemed daring things to have on your roof—actually inviting the lightning to strike at you. I kept my distance.

Summers came and went, and I took a passing interest in radios and electricity and learned that the earth itself was part of an electrical system so vast that it could absorb without a murmur all the volts heaven poured into it. So I was disposed to listen when, on a July day years later in New Hampshire, a car climbed the grass-spined gravel road of the old farmhouse we were restoring and a man from the lightning-rod company climbed out. He said he'd heard we were working on the house and barn. We sat for a time in the shade of the massive ash tree on the lawn, chatting about the weather and the porcupines and where to get a granite front step and whether Chester Atwood was ever going to sell his filling station down in the Flat. Finally he got around to talking about lightning rods.

It might have been his quickest sale, except that I made him explain how the whole system worked. He told me that the rods themselves needed to stand straight up from chimneys and gables and that the sharper they were the better they would attract the lightning. He explained the need for the long metal ground stake, driven deep beside the foundation to disperse the lightning into the earth. And he sang the virtues of the heavy copper cable his company used. It needed to be thick and strong, he said; it had to bear up over the years without breaking or corroding through. Nothing worse, he said, than attracting all that energy and giving it no place to go.

I agreed. So a few weeks later he was clambering along the shingles and fixing us up with a set of rods. He even put a couple on our much-prized ash tree—showing us the scarred bark where, in years past, lightning had raced down it. "Maybe it'll get hit again, maybe not," he said. "This way, it don't hardly matter whether't does or doesn't."

Summers being what they are, it wasn't long before we had a chance to test his workmanship. One hot, still afternoon the breeze sprang up more suddenly than it should have, flipping up the undersides of the poplar leaves beyond the stone wall. The sky behind the barn went devil-black. We heard the distant thunder and gathered in the garden tools before the first fat plops of rain danced in the marigolds along the walk and filled the house with the smell of damp earth as we went about shutting windows.

Then came the deluge, and the crack and dazzle of the storm tearing into the tree and the chimney stacks above us. Hovering overhead for what seemed like hours, it seemed almost to know of our new-laid copper taunt. The rain turned to hail. The lightning blasted away at everything upright. More than once the flash and roar came right together. More than once the telephone, sitting beside the wooden box with the black crank for calling the operator, jangled furiously and seemed to leap across the table. We heard, later, of phone poles knocked sideways down in the Flat, of trees cracked open and branches lying in the roads. But up on our hillside, house and barn and ash tree stood unruffled, as though nothing had happened. Maybe they got hit repeatedly. Maybe they went untouched. We could never tell; it hardly seemed to matter.

In the summers of a life that has since taken us far beyond New Hampshire, I've thought more than once about that farm. And again and again, when the pressure builds on the hot and muggy afternoons of the soul and life seems hopelessly exposed, I recall my talk with that salesman. He didn't say a word about running away from the storms. He just talked about driving the groundstake deep into the earth. He talked about putting up good strong cable and keeping it well connected to that foundation. And he talked about using sharp rods, set upright on the highest pinnacle you can reach. Maybe they'll get hit, and maybe not. Either way, as he said, it don't hardly matter.

THE
ICE OF
NECESSITY

☐

Not so many years ago, when refrigerators were still called iceboxes, we started summering on an island in the Canadian bush. At the end of our lake was a fishing camp and store, back of which was an ice house. It was a squat building nestled among trees, and it had an inner and outer wall with some kind of local insulation—sawdust, maybe—in between.

In June, when the campers first arrived, it was full from floor to ceiling with clear, black blocks carefully packed in snow. The place down the highway packed theirs in sawdust, and you had to hose them off before you used them. Ours was better: it came out clean. In June you opened the thick double doors and found, dark and solemn, a wall of ice. By August you could step inside and close the doors. Fishermen sometimes put a couple of pickerel in there to keep until they caught enough to clean, laying them flat on the waist-high shelves formed by selling off the upper blocks.

In those days the ice came out of the lake, which froze so thick that the trucks used it as a road to the logging camps back in the woods. Of course there was electricity in the store and freezers that could have made ice by the ton. But these blocks were natural. They cut them right at the end of the dock.

I remember, one summer, looking out at the water which six months before had been frozen solid. How much to know, I thought, about cutting ice. I'd seen the saws they used—two-handed affairs with teeth like the back of a brontosaurus. Whoever did it had to know just how to use those saws. And they had to know when—not before the ice was thick enough to make worthwhile blocks, nor after it was too deep to cut. Did they start with a pick or an auger, I wondered. And how did they cut the pattern in order to get the most blocks with the fewest cuts and still not fall in? No doubt they trained the youngsters in the finer points. "Someday," they would have said, "you'll have to do this for yourselves."

But someday came and went, and when I was last there I bought ice from a machine. I didn't see the ice house. The blocks were in plastic bags, clean, easy to carry. They came in by truck from the city and were stored in a steel cooler.

Well, no wonder, I thought. Nowadays the highway is a busy place all winter, and time, which used to hang heavily over a landscape that darkened by mid-afternoon, skips along to the steady pace of truckers and travelers. Time is tending the store, not cutting ice. The delivery truck from the city probably plies a weekly route, and the ice man fills the cooler himself, watching the supply.

Convenient, too: You grab the plastic bag by its tied-off ear and away you go without so much as a drip.

And that's progress. So why did I feel this twinge of regret, of nostalgia? After all, ice is ice—frozen water, as pure in the city as off the dock. Any way you make it it keeps the butter hard and chills the cream.

I grabbed my perfectly good block of ice by the ear and shuffled off, mumbling to myself about being too sentimental. But on the way to the dock I had another thought. I had two miles of water to cross in a small motor-boat. I was going to get wet from the spray, no doubt about it. If there had been a paved road up to our cabin, I should have taken it, stepping dryly from the car into the kitchen with my dry block of ice.

But there wasn't. And for the first time, I realized that I was grateful not to have that opportunity. I was glad to be protected from convenience. For convenience, I thought, is a great insulator; and the price we pay for its insulation is a loss of contact with and commitment to our environment. I was going to get cold and wet, drenched by a lake that over the years had made itself almost a part of me. Convenience had provided me with no alternatives: I had to take the lake and its weathers pretty much on its own terms.

I looked at my shining ice-block as we slapped along over the water, and I saw then what had troubled me. It was the subtle, almost invisible shift of attitudes brought on by the pressure toward convenience. I would no longer go to the store with a sense of delight in the old tradition of ice-cutting—in which, in however small a way, I was about to participate. The good people at the store would no longer be selling their ice with quiet pride—the way the man down the road sells cucumbers and tomatoes at his own stand. They would sell it casually, the way you would sell a bottle of soda or someone else's packaged donuts.

That, it seems, is a pretty stiff price to pay for convenience. No longer attached tightly to the land, the place, the seasons, we have carefully labored to insulate ourselves from them. So we no longer know, nor care for, the processes that produce the things we need to live by. Our hand is apart from its works; we live indifferently, aloof, in the coolers of our modern cities.

Or so we think, in our nostalgic moments. And then, like a glorious reminder, something happens. It snows three feet, or the power goes off, or the gas supply runs short, or the supermarket runs out of bread. And suddenly we're thrown back on our own devices: we shovel out our neighbors, lend candles, share fireplaces, eat our friend's baking. From being isolated, insulated individuals, we warm to a spontaneous commitment against adversity. As our conveniences slip away, we find an old resourcefulness free of these dependencies, a resourcefulness that once again cuts the ice of necessity from the great clear lake of the spirit.

EMILY
UP
THE
STREET

☐

There are some who can say, quite honestly, that they've always loved poetry. From their earliest whimpering, it seems, they thought in rhythms and saw a world shimmering with symbols.

I've always been in awe of such people. I had an unexceptionally boyish upbringing, doing boyish things among the barns and slingshots and model airplanes of rural Massachusetts. Poetry, which came into my life sideways and rather late, never really had a chance. For a long time, I must have looked at it pretty much the way a grazing cow looks at a rock: with no annoyance, but feeling that without it there might be a little more grass.

Or so I have always thought. Recently, however, I have begun to wonder why, in soil so ill prepared, my interest in poetry should ever have taken root. Strange to say, I think it had something to do with the fact that I had to walk to school.

Our house lay some three-quarters of a mile from the chunky brick school buildings up near the center of the town of Amherst. For all that distance, however, it was but nine doors away. Going up the hill from our house, you passed five of those doors within two blocks. From there on only four houses remained. By the time I came along, their owners had let trees and hedges grow up along the road, making a kind of extended woods running most of the way to school.

And did I, like Wordsworth among his daffodils, wander lonely as a cloud through these groves, composing in my head the mighty line? I did not. I scampered through them with my third-grade pals, hurling horse chestnuts at unsuspecting second-graders and whacking tree trunks with sticks plucked up from among the leaves.

No, we never thought much about language. But it was there. The fluffy stuff that drifted from trees and blew about like tangled yarn we called "wiggilotti," probably because it reminded us of wigs. And the best of the sticks—the stoutest and most readily wielded—we dignified with the mysterious name of "cudgels." It glorified our afternoons, that language, even if we couldn't have said how.

And always there was the most intriguing house—brick, tightly hedged, and perched atop a hill. Surrounded by gardens, it was bathed in an aura of its own, something that made us hold it in certain reverence. "That," we had been told from our earliest infant strollerings, "is the Emily Dickinson house."

In those acorn days, I hadn't an idea who she was. Our teachers never took us there, never went out of their way to tell us about her uniqueness or her reclusiveness or the brilliant cameos of insight in her poems. A prophet is not without honor, as my father used to say, save in his own country. We lived with her as with the hitching posts still planted here and there throughout the town—mindful of their antiquity, but heedless of the bygone culture they reflected.

So it was not until I was in graduate school, immersed in poetry, that I drifted into an acquaintance with her. My parents, having sold our old home and not yet moved into another, lived for a year in the Emily Dickinson house. I remember visiting them one winter weekend. Climbing the stairs to my frosty corner bedroom, I mapped my way among literary coordinates grown almost to the proportion of myth: Richard Wilbur's poem about Emily Dickinson's cupola, her own poems about books like frigates and liquor never brewed, and, next to mine, her room, sparsely furnished and with her own dress still hanging in the closet.

I saw vividly on that visit how poetry works. It was not just her accuracy, not just that she had touched on the same robins and roses, the same clouds and winds, that still covered my boyhood a century after she saw them. Nor was it simply that her words had found in them a life, a significance, which as a boy I had dimly sensed but never articulated. I saw it most clearly, I remember, as I stepped out into her garden after lunch on that gray Sunday. The sun, having fought clouds since it came up beyond the Pelham Hills, had nearly given up, and the day was darkening. Her words, echoing the New England Calvinism of her age, fairly glowed in my memory:

> There's a certain slant of light,
> Winter afternoons,
> That oppresses, as the heft
> Of cathedral tunes.

The light was there, and the mood, and the age—all wrapped up in the words and the garden. And there, too—inexplicably, as poetry so often does it—was the delight. There, in the face of oppression and heaviness, was a statement so exact, so powerful, that it registered for me not sorrow but an odd and paradoxical joy—joy in the fact that language works, joy in the fact that I had seen it work, joy in the sudden discovery of why that house had always held for us its special aura. And joy that, after so many years, I had at last met the long-lost neighbor up the street.

NIBBLING
AT
SHAKESP.

□

This year the first day of summer, drifting through the treetops from the hills beyond the lake, again caught me by surprise. I always vow to have finished spring's tasks before it arrives—to have swished the cobwebs from the rafters, washed the rainstreaks from the windows, swept up the seed-husks left beneath the wood stove by the wintering mice. But the solstice always finds me half unbuttoned. There are, of course, so many fine excuses. This year it was the rain and the delicious indoor afternoons, cozy with books, rocking themselves away before the fire. On such days one can forgive any number of cobwebs.

So it wasn't until a sunny morning well past midsummer's eve that I cast a critical eye on the small two-window shed that serves as my warm-weather study. I had been reading a particularly fine essay on the relationship of architecture to serious book-reading—complete with asides about the invention of bookshelves, and the need for domestic silence and solitude, and Montaigne's library in his round tower—when the spring-cleanerly spirit descended upon me. Rag in hand, I attacked the broad plywood desktop, flailed the dust from the window screens, and whisked the floor. And at last I turned to the bookshelves.

I had built them some years before out of plain pine and common nails, and each summer had stocked them with the raw materials for whatever research project was under way. But for several years, as our family had moved about, they had stood empty. Looking at them, I remembered the boxes of books still in storage up in the barn. Now, I thought, it's time.

"O, Dad!" my daughters chorused in near-unison, "doweHAVta?" But they had both come of readerly age, and a little logic convinced them that there might be something in those boxes to whet their appetites. Pretty soon they showed up at the door of my study, puffing under the weight of well-taped movers' boxes labeled "Novel: James to Hem." and "lit. crit." and "16th C." Then they left, and the morning wore on, and I labored in silent chaos. For no book-lover, I suspect, can simply open one box of books at a time. No, they must *all* be sampled, all emptied and stacked precariously on chairs and tables and floor, all handled and pondered and reordered and relived on their way to the shelf. Midway through my toil, resting on a box labeled "antiques, etc"— which would shortly yield up a leather-bound copy of Whittier's *Snow-Bound* and Volume V of the lavishly illustrated *Botanical Magazine;* or, *Flower-Garden Displayed* (London, 1792)—I fell into a chapter-long conversation with Jane Austen's Emma, still "handsome,

clever, and rich . . . with very little to distress or vex her."
Leaning idly against the window jamb, I lost myself in
Newland Archer's biting remarks on nineteenth-century
New York society in Edith Wharton's *The Age of Inno-
cence.* Finally, knife in hand, I slit the tape on the box
labeled "Shakesp."

I thought as I opened it that something was amiss.
The books were there, all right: small blue-bound copies
of the Yale Shakespeare, paperback critical studies, a
couple of biographies. But the ones on top had an odd
patina of dust. Here and there, as I delved deeper, tiny
flakes of paper fluttered about. At last, in a corner
under G. Wilson Knight's *The Crown of Life,* I found
the conclusive evidence: a heap of paper scraps littered
with acorn shells, the work, no doubt, of a family of red
squirrels.

Why they had chosen to nest with the Bard, I don't
know. Their taste, however, was elegant. Ignoring lesser
plays and modern commentaries, they had confined
themselves to the sonnets and to *King Lear.* In deference,
no doubt, to my scholarly impecuniosity, they had settled
for paperbacks. Yet how disappointing must have been
their efforts! Limiting themselves to the upper margins
of Lear, they had barely nibbled Edmund's soliloquy
on "the excellent foppery of the world"—and never
even touched Lear's tempestuous battles with the winter
storms. They plunged deeper into the sonnets, yet
seemed to have fared the worse. There, in the sourest
tradition of the pedant, they munched dutifully through
the introduction. Then they devoured the footnotes of the
first six sonnets—and never once tasted the poetry itself.
With an irony worthy of Petrarch, they had played

out their hibernation in a rabble of undigested scholar-ship—while, inches away, the courtly pentameter of Sonnet 6 began:

Then let not winter's ragged hand deface
In thee thy summer ere thou be distilled.

Musing on all that, I finished putting my books in order—even the two gnawed ones. Their spines were intact, so I shelved them along with the others. Now and then, as I glance at them, I think about this thing called reading—how delicate an art it really is, how it must be nurtured and nested, and how we acquire our taste for it in the long winter nights of the heart. And now and then, as I walk about the woods among a scurry of squirrels, I wonder what they make of Shakespeare. Do they, like students sadly mistaught, think of him as nothing but a hard slog through stifling verbiage? Would they have gone farther if they had ignored the footnotes and plunged unaided into the glorious text itself? What if they'd taken their first serious bites among Fitzgerald, or Hardy, or Sinclair Lewis—would that have lured them backward into the classics, or dulled their budding tastes?

They chatter at me from behind the paper birches, but I can't make out what they're saying. They sound like literary critics—deconstructionists maybe?

ALL
OVER
GULPY

☐

In the end, it became a habit. I would come in late from an autumn evening out with friends—the large, dark house drifting toward silence, my parents asleep upstairs, and the thousand thoughts of a fifteen-year-old still racing through my mind. Pausing in the kitchen, I would mix a can of tuna with celery and mayonnaise. Then I would head for bed. There we would sit, the cat and I, huddled against the pillows in the only pool of light in the house, eating tuna from a bowl and letting the day subside.

And reading. In those days I never thought of myself as a literary type. I was, as they say, "into" the sciences; and a world of *things,* each solid and compelling in the as-yet-unchallenged assumption of its ultimate reality, filled my days. The symbols that mattered were not words. They were the hieroglyphs of the logarithmic tables, the schematics of electrical circuits, the elements of the periodic table. So I never thought to excuse myself for what I read. Others my age, long immersed in words, had seized on Dickens and Dostoyevsky, Kafka and Camus. Not I. In perfect unconcern for the proprieties of the educated mind, I read and reread "Pogo."

I couldn't have said why. Part of it, I suppose, has to do with a teen-ager's curious blend of the eight-year-old and the adult. Maybe reading the cartoon antics of Walt Kelly's swamp animals was something of a throwback, a habit never quite outgrown. Whatever the reason, I would pick up those well-tattered books and dip into them at random—swept instantly into sequences of frames that were at the same time entirely familiar, eminently predictable, and invariably hilarious.

Nor was I alone. Winters, my father and sister would chuckle over "Pogo" in front of the fire. Summers, the dozens of pogoisms we had absorbed would fix themselves in our vocabulary. In those days we were busy building a summer cottage on an almost-uninhabited Canadian lake. We improvised many things—the peeled spruce poles for the roof-beams, the names of uncharted bays and islands, the very language with which we conveyed our experience. And what a pogoesque tongue it was! "Aaargh!" we would exclaim in frustration, echoing Albert Alligator's bold-faced capitals. "Gormy" came to characterize bad weather. We named our canoe "Gulpy," recollecting that once Pogo's friend Churchy Lafemme, moved to sobs by some touching occasion, had said, "I come all over gulpy." We even appropriated— don't ask why—another of Albert's great growls ("Rowr!") and, adding to it the Latin word ("Esox") for one of the fish that abounded in our lake, christened our camp "Esox Rowr."

Why that fascination with "Pogo"? What did a strip now remembered largely for a single aphorism—"We have met the enemy, and they is us"—have in it, that it could so shape a family's entire discourse?

I puzzled over that question for years—until, the other day, I found I could put it off no longer. So, finding that my original copies of the Pogo books had (as they say here in New England) "come up missin'," I settled down one afternoon in the Boston Public Library to renew my acquaintance.

The librarian, looking only slightly askance at my request, went off to fetch me a half-dozen Pogo books. Waiting for her at an oak table among the marble statues and statue-quiet scholars of that somber, vault-ceilinged reading room, I thought of the hundreds of hours I'd spent since my teen-age years in libraries like this one. Somewhere along the way, things had given way to words. Since my last reading of "Pogo," I had abandoned my chemistry set and my electronic gear and found my way into literature. The intervening years had filled themselves with James Joyce and Dylan Thomas, Wallace Stevens and E. E. Cummings—wordsmiths all, shaping their words as a cabinetmaker does his wood and tossing them, juggler-wise, into the air in hilarious sleight of hand. For them, I had learned, words were truly things.

Suddenly, to the sound of the librarian's retreating step, the familiar books were before me. I opened one cautiously—fearing that in the end they would prove merely silly, simple-minded, superficial. And as I steeled myself against disappointment, my eyes fell on the familiar frames—and Beauregard Hound and Howland Owl and old Sarcophagus MacAbre and Wiley Cat, and Snavely the snake ("harmless nor a caterpiggle"), and Ma'm'selle Hepzibah with whom Pogo himself was perpetually falling in love, all surged into life. There was that onomatopoeia with its almost medieval vigor: Albert grunting *mmph-stbbt! grsr-yeep!* as he lifted heavy loads, Pogo grumbling *moomph!* and *growmp!* in fits of jealousy. There was that silly boat, always with a different name and always tipping over in mid-sentence. It was all, in Pogo's word, "DEE-licorice."

And there, too, was something I had always sensed but never recognized: the mind of a wordsmith so in love with language that even in his silliest moments he sang with an almost Joycean energy. It was in the names, like Churchy Lafemme (*cherchez la femme,* as the French say) and Howland (Howling) Owl. It was in the speeches: "Is you gonna volunteer," says Pogo to Churchy in an interchange spoofing man-made pollution, "to be the First to *suicidelicately sacerfice* hisself to clear the polluters, *human beans,* from the earth?" And it was all matched with that tremendous vitality of line, flowing from a bottomless font of wit and a love of incongruity.

Now, I am a restrained man. I am not given to outbursts. I hold libraries in high regard. But right there, amid the stares of those marble busts and the silence of scholarship, I exploded into laughter. Try as I would, I could not contain it: it was as though, after all those years, cat and tuna and "Pogo" were all reassembled, and I was alone again in that swampy and delightful world.

With a difference. This time, I knew why I was reading—knew, at last, that of the manifold influences along
my path from things into words, that habit of "Pogo" had
mattered as much as any.

STONE
AGAINST
CHAOS

☐

To my teenage eye, the house was gloriously authentic. It had perched on a ridge of the Pelham Hills since the seventeenth century, when that part of Massachusetts was still the frontier and the land gave unsparingly of rock and timber. The old boys who built it, using the natural insulation of earth and stone, dug it so deeply into a sloping hillside that the first and second stories both opened out at ground level on different sides. They had sheathed it with narrow clapboards and chimneyed it with a massive structure of narrow bricks, complete with beehive oven and multiple fireplaces. Through small, many-paned windows of rippled glass, the sun warmed the floorboards and wainscoting, so that a reddish-brown glow seemed to rise from some translucent depth within the pine.

In decor as well as structure, it fairly seethed with character. There was pewter on the sideboard, and a small doorbell fastened to a curlicue of metal that sprang to life at the slightest touch. There was a blackened iron-crane mounted above the hearth, ceiling beams hung with herbs and kettles and baskets, and wrought-iron latches worked easily through worn holes in the doors. It was all of a piece, with a pattern and design of its own, and everything had its place.

Behind the house were several outbuildings. One of them, similarly carved into a hillside, was a modest storage shed almost hidden by bushes. It had stone foundation walls on three sides, a rough-board front, and a peaked roof that sat level with the hillside at the rear and stood well above your head over the door. Inside, the lower stones near the dirt floor were beaded with dampness from springs in the ground above, keeping it cool and earth-scented even on the sultriest days.

To further insulate it, the builders had planted an oak on the hill above. It was now a mammoth tree, with limb and leaf so tightly woven that the sun never once peeked through from June until October. It also had mammoth roots, which is why I was there that summer morning.

"You see that rear wall?" said Al, who owned the farm and who looked to be less than half an age removed from those original builders. Propping the door open for light, he shuffled into the dankness.

"See how she's bowed right out?" he said, carving a gentle convexity in the air with a gnarled hand. "That's the roots behind, pushing on her." My job, he explained, was to remove the center portion of rocks, chop out the offending dirt and roots, and rebuild the wall. There was a solid beam stretching from corner to corner above the rock wall, he noted, so the roof wouldn't come down while I was working.

31

I didn't know much about drywalls—he'd hired me that summer to cut grass and putter around the garden at his wife's behest—but I didn't see there was much to it. "Just do the best you can," he said, with a knowing smile.

It didn't occur to me at the time that those words carried any deep significance. I got the old iron pry-bar and the pick and shovel and the wheelbarrow, and took off my shirt and set to work. The stones ranged in size from small hams to nail kegs, and came out easily: They'd been gradually dislodging themselves for decades, and were pretty near ready to tumble down on their own. I had them out in about an hour. By noon I'd cut back the earth enough so that I judged the stones would set up smooth and flush when I put them back.

So after lunch I tied a string tight from corner to corner and began rebuilding—turning each stone to find its best face, hefting it into place, jiggling it around until it just touched the string, and chinking up the holes with little rocks. I'd noticed that the original builders had put the larger stones near the bottom, so I did that, too. But it was only as I approached the upper beam, and eyeballed the remaining stones, that I saw there would be a couple of big ones left over.

That's funny, I thought. I had figured this to be a kind of natural jigsaw puzzle, where everything had its place and you just had to find the right slot. But when the puzzle was complete, there were the spare pieces.

I opened the door good and wide and stood back to study my handiwork. And that's when I noticed something else. You could run your eye right along the side walls from front to back, following a single layer of stones all the way. You could turn the corner, and trace the same straight, level lines across the back—until you got to my part of the wall. Then the lines dissolved, fracturing into a hodgepodge of crooked stones pointing every which-way. What's more, the side walls were close fitting and tight, while my part of the back looked distinctly more porous.

The more I studied it, the worse it seemed. It wasn't that it was badly done: it was flush with the string, and it was tucked up tight under the beam to support the roof, and it certainly wasn't going anywhere. It was just that something wasn't right.

I cleaned up and went to find Al. He poked his head in and was quiet for a moment.

"You can tell where I rebuilt it," I offered hesitantly. He nodded, going over to the corner to squint along it.

"That's good," he finally said. "That'll stay there awhile." As he was leaving, he shot me a quiet grin. "You did the best you could."

I suppose it's still standing. That was three decades ago, and I've never been back to look. I knew Al for years afterwards, and he never said anything more about it. He was right. Being what I was, what else could I have done—the hapless child of the age of the backhoes and bulldozers that had conquered the wilderness spreading westward for thousands of miles beyond the Pelham Hills?

I think of those old boys now and then, when the pulse and pressure of our quick-built age wells up in my life. I think of them building for the long haul—for their grandchildren, for a nation still unformed from a new continent, for a future they cared deeply about. For them, a sense of pattern was neither a luxury nor a burden. It must have been something internal—some intuition, as they studied the rocks already set up and the ones still to go, that within the manifest chaos of the world there was a discoverable order.

Maybe, like their stonework, they saw themselves as bulwarks against that chaos. Maybe they sensed a deeper purpose, served not only by building level and true but by crafting every part of their life with an innate design. Maybe, in the end, they left us less with a collection of antiques than with a set of intrinsic convictions—that, even in their least public places, function never should overrule form, and that foundation ultimately determines superstructure. Maybe they saw something we've almost forgotten: that what you are when nobody's looking is what you really are.

NEW ENGLAND
WHEN IT
RUNS

□

The other day somebody asked me why I liked New England. Having no direct answer to hand, I burst into anecdote. I'm not sure my interlocutor understood me—nor, in the end, that I understood myself. Let me try again.

At that impressionable age when romance exceeds rationality—known among university educators as the sophomore year—I found myself in want of a car. I had even saved up a few hundred dollars when, one balmy summer day, a newspaper ad caught my eye. On offer was no mere Chevy hard-top, nor even a snappy little Triumph. For sale, at what I now see was a dangerously low price, was a seven-year-old Jaguar two-seater.

I suppose I was lost from the moment I read the description: convertible, varnished wood dashboard, wire wheels with knock-off hubs, newly repainted. Even the color seized my naive and adjectival heart: British Racing Green, conjuring up images of tweedy aristocrats and high speeds. The thought that such a machine might actually be mine rendered all other ads illegible.

For a while, of course, reason lobbied with sober thoughts about Nash Ramblers and Plymouth Sedans. I think I even imagined, when I set out to see the Jaguar, that I was under no obligation. So it was with a studied aloofness that I ran my hand over the leather seat-back, examined the chrome camshaft cover, and grasped the sturdy four-speed shift lever. The owner put down the top and handed me the keys. I slid in and turned it over, watching the tachometer spring up into the idle range, hearing the throb of the twin exhausts. Pretending a skil-fulness beyond my years, I put it in gear, revved the engine, and let out the clutch. Whereupon, with a violent jerk and a spurt of pebbles, I was flattened against the seat-back and catapulted up the street. In that swirl of leaves and dust, my aloofness vanished.

So, from that moment, did my peace of mind. For I suppose it's fair to say that I never really did get control of that car. It had its own temperament, it seemed, and set its own priorities. It could be scintillating, provocative, allur-ing, and altogether wonderful: hugging the road on cor-ners, darting away from stop signs, and always delivering more power than you could quite manage. It was, as Shakespeare said in another context, "such stuff as dreams are made on," providing more metaphors for experience than a dozen poets could digest. A two-seater, it had no room for extra baggage. Full of pep, it expressed a constant longing to be somewhere else. Sitting in the parking lot during the week, it seemed almost to cry out its rebuke of the sedentary, scholarly life. Yet it had its own intellectual structure. Its central lesson, I think, was the same as that taught by any serious engagement with the life of the mind: that not only the goal, but the getting there, was exhilarating. Some cars are mere nouns. That one was pure verb.

If it rode in clouds of glory, however, it was also possessed of monumental faults. The least was its lack of insulation: I recall a memorable ride down the New York Thruway one winter night when our only recourse from the freezing gales came from stuffing the contents of my laundry bag into the cracks around the windows. More serious was the state of its electrical system, so corroded that at times the left-turn signal set all the parking lights flashing. Its front suspension could only be remedied by replacing two Y-shaped pieces of steel at a hundred dollars apiece. It ultimately lost most of its oil pressure. And for some reason never wholly clear, it ran on the hot side. On long trips the floorboards under the passenger seat would become positively untouchable. Any girl unfortunate enough to ride there on a humid evening came away resembling a poached salmon.

All of these things I strove to remedy. But if it is true (as yachtsmen say) that a boat is a hole in the water surrounded by wood into which one pours money, it is equally true that an old sports car is the fiscal equivalent of a black hole in space. Any amount of money, orbiting too close to it, disappears instantly and without a trace. I kept it for barely a year, selling it for half what I had paid and still owing the garage for some parts.

Was it worth it? That's what I was getting at in answering the question about New England. Dear old New England! I've had a lover's quarrel with it for years. I know it's miserably cold in winter, steamy in summer. I know it's stubborn, willful, backward-looking, pedantic, aloof—full of ghastly politics and stunning hypocrisies. And yet, and yet—what could I say to such a question? I answered by recalling that, when I could have had any of the duller and more responsible cars, I bought an old sports car. It was full of power. It was loaded with options. It came with all the authority of tradition. And it was beautifully designed. It would leave all the competition in the dust—if only it could be made to run.

I sold the car. But I don't suppose I'll ever leave New England.

WAYS
TO BUY
NAILS

□

You must understand, first, that I'm not wild about shopping. Haberdashers, stationers, gift shops, fish markets, perfumeries, confectioneries—I'm grateful they're there, but I try to keep my distance. For one sort of shop, however, I have a peculiar weakness: that catchall emporium of tools, paints, and kitchen supplies known as the small-town hardware store.

My fondness began early, when as a small boy I'd go with my parents to a place rather grandly known as The Mutual Plumbing and Heating Company. Up front it was all light bulbs and lunch pails, candles and clothespins and can openers and everything else now called "housewares." But out in the back there were lengths of threaded iron pipe racked beside coils of electrical cable and the green-edged glow of window glass. Up front, the Mutual smelled of plastic and soap; back there, it smelled of cup grease and turpentine, laced now and then with the scent of pine and cedar and the faint oily-iron tang of new nails.

It's the nails, after all, that make a hardware store. Nowadays, all sorts of stores will sell you hammers and angle irons and little boxes of screws. But only true hardware stores have nails in bulk. In that respect, Mutual was the genuine article. Its gunmetal-gray bins, deep and open-fronted and upward-sloping, held what to my child's eye was a world of nails. There were box nails and common nails, roofing nails and wallboard nails, ring-shanks that you couldn't pull out and forty-penny spikes that you could hardly drive in, delicate finishing nails and double-headed scaffolding nails and square-cut flooring nails and blue-black shingle nails—a universe as varied as humanity itself, and adapted to its thousand needs.

Somewhere in the bins was a kind of short-handled Neptune's trident used for clawing the nails into brown paper bags. You put the bag on the scale hanging from a nearby beam, its metal pan suspended from chains like an upside-down Quaker bonnet. If a clerk were around, he'd mark up the price in grease pencil on the rolled-over bag; if not, they'd trust you to tell them over at the cash register. And if, like me, you were too short to see into the scale-pan, you could always stand on one of the short wooden kegs, labeled *clous* and *fabriqué au Canada,* that squatted nearby on the worn plank floor.

Mutual moved, and I grew up. But I find I've not outgrown my love of hardware stores. Maybe that's why I like our small Maine town. It's blessed with two such stores—in which, at some point each weekend, I can usually be found.

The uninitiated, no doubt, will ask why one patronizes *two* such stores. Surely one is enough. And so it is—if all you want to do is buy hardware. These two, however, are more than stores. Each, in its own way, is a kind of window on the world. They're the living embodiments of two entirely opposite philosophies, two polar ways of looking at life.

On the surface, of course, they don't look all that different. The one "downstreet" (as they say in these parts) is sandwiched between a toy shop and a grocery store that still delivers, and it's partial to housewares. The other, sprawling out behind an old clapboard house on the edge of the town, turns progressively into a lumber-yard with every step you take toward the rear. But both sell the basics: if you're after pie plates or stove bolts, either one will do. And both have charge accounts—which, in the manner of Yankee rurality, are set up when the store owner writes down your name and address and, with a couple of well-placed questions, satisfies himself as to which house you live in.

Then wherein the difference? The evidence is in the nails—not in what they are (each store carries about the same), but in how they're sold. Downtown, the nails are right under the counter by the cash register. At the other place, the nails are out in the back by themselves.

Outsiders, used to more urban ways, might conclude that this distinction points to a matter of trust—that the downstreet store keeps a more watchful eye on something so eminently portable and pocketable. After months of offhand study, I'm led to a different hypothesis. I think that just as anthropologists distinguish between hunting and gathering societies, so one can distinguish two different clientele for these stores: the hunters and, for want of a better word, the askers.

The lumberyard store caters to the former. It assumes that its patrons will hunt down, unassisted, whatever they're after. It's a place where, all by yourself, you set out to stalk the odd-sized furniture clamp, search out the coil of three-wire twelve-gauge cable, and track down the final can of forest-green spray enamel. There are clerks, to be sure—affable folks, learned in their trade, and willing to spend a lot of time in their helpfulness. But they always seem to be helping someone else. It's the kind of store to visit when you know exactly what you want—or when, as often happens, you long for a little quiet space to mull over your options and browse unmolested for something that might come in handy.

Things are not like that downstreet. You can hardly cross the threshold without being greeted—by name, if you've been there often enough. Most things are shelved in the open. But it seems somehow proper to let the clerk show you to the right shelf. It's the kind of store you visit when you don't know enough to know what to ask for—or when, in the long and racking reaches of some recalcitrant basement project, you simply need to commiserate with another understanding heart.

And that, after all, is what shopping is all about. It's not just what you're buying. It's how you're buying it. There are times, for all of us, when even the purchase of a pound of nails is an act of uncertainty—or an admission of failure, or a patient bowing to duty. And then there are times when that same purchase, in the zest of a project well-launched, is a soaring declaration of self-reliance, dominion, and exultation. There's a time for hunting and a time for asking—a time for being left alone, and a time for the comfort of helpfulness. Which is why, I guess, there will always be more than one way to buy nails.

WHEN YOU
TRAVEL
ALONE

☐

That November afternoon, the white clapboard houses on Masonic Street stood prosperous and alone on their century-old foundations—decently cordial, I sensed, but slightly disapproving as I once again pulled the car up in front of number forty-five. This was a house, after all, not quite like the others. The paint, after years of Maine sea-coast winters, was beginning to peel. The once-decorative plantings now owed more to natural inclination than human shears. The new-made railing along the steps down to the street was a humble, workmanlike affair of two-by-fours.

"Come up," she said when I poked my head into the dim hallway and called. I climbed the narrow stairs, past the steam radiator on the ground floor, past the now-antique, red-glass-shaded lamp suspended from its long chain, past the newly plastered upstairs ceiling re-paired by volunteers from the local trade school when it fell in last year. As usual, she was in her easy chair by the sunny window—a diminutive woman in a flowered dress, sitting in the very room where, late in the last century, she had been born.

Much had changed since then. The fireplace beside her had been bricked up. The old family piano had been moved into her room. A telephone had been installed within reach. Other changes hadn't stuck: a 1950s wooden television cabinet, still sitting in a commanding position, was empty of its electronics and slowly filling with books and magazines. She doesn't seem to miss it, I thought as I headed for the chair opposite her. True to form, the pile of newspapers at her right hand was well-turned. I hadn't gotten my coat off before she said, "What about all that excitement in the election!"

So we chatted about the large turnout, and what it meant up in our town that they hadn't passed the new school—she'd been a teacher all her working life—and what it meant for George Bush at midterm. And then the conversation drifted toward Thanksgiving.

Growing up, she recalled, they had a family of nine for Thanksgiving dinners. She talked about preparing the fruit pies and jam tarts days ahead, and then the vegetables, and then finally the turkey. And about the tales of family history: how her grandfather would talk about the Civil War, where he served in a balloon regiment that did aerial reconnaissance behind enemy lines, and how he later turned up in a photograph by Mathew Brady; how her father, a lawyer, would recall studying oratory up in Bangor with Hannibal Hamlin, who had been Abraham Lincoln's vice-president; how her mother's side of the family was related to Nathaniel Hawthorne.

And here I am, I thought, sitting in the last decade of the twentieth century talking to someone who knows, at only second-hand, what it was like to fight in the Civil War. And yet I sensed that there had been in her life an inner stirring—or maybe an inner peace—that had prevented her from becoming stuck in the merely historical. It hadn't been easy—not for the young girl who once won the Solid Gold Prize in her Sunday School because, as she told me with a chuckle, she had "a fly-paper memory" and could answer any question of Biblical fact they threw at her. It was a memory still unclouded. Then how, I found myself wondering, can she have avoided becoming a slave to it? How could someone with so rich a heritage in the past live so contentedly in the present—alone and uncomplaining, generous of heart, and utterly unmoved by the sentimentality of recollected affection?

She must have read my unspoken question—though, when she first took up her tale, I wasn't sure it was going to be an answer. "I've had turkey every Thanksgiving Day of my life," she began, "except once." I settled back to listen.

Though plenty of young men had been interested in her when she was growing up, she had never married. So when her mother died, she said, she was left alone here in the big family house. She was tempted to feel sorry for herself, especially on holidays. But she found a friend who went with her each Thanksgiving Day to one of the nearby hotels for dinner. Came the day one year, however, and the weather was horrible—such wind, cold, and sleeting rain that even the short walk downtown was out of the question. "Well, I had nothing in the refrigerator for dinner," she said. Dejected and forlorn, she sat down alone to a meal of scrambled eggs.

But as she started eating, she said, she began to think about the meaning of Thanksgiving. And she started counting things she was thankful for.

"What were they?" I asked.

"Well, I remember being grateful that I had a roof over my head," she answered, "and that I had enough clothes to dress myself—though I wasn't a great hand for putting on style—and that I had money enough to buy the food I needed.

"And do you know, when I was finished," she declared, "I felt just as good as if I had had a whole turkey dinner!" That was years ago, she added, and since then she'd never had any trouble being alone.

She fell quiet. It was one of those moments that come now and then even to the most seasoned interviewers—times when you wish you could freeze the conversation, sit in silence, simply let the meaning reverberate and build its own ramifications.

But there was something else to be asked. "What would you say to somebody—right now, in 1990—who's tempted to feel alone, separate from family and from friends on Thanksgiving Day?" I asked. "What's it *feel* like not to feel alone?"

She paused for a moment. And then simply, in the matter-of-fact way you might tell someone what you thought about a political candidate or a new pie recipe, she said: "I think I'm companioned by the Lord. I don't feel any sense of being alone. I feel a sense of security—the same as you had with your parents when you went round with them or got in bed with them.

"You know," she added reflectively, with the hint of a smile playing on her lips, "when you travel alone you travel farthest."

There was a different kind of sunlight in the street as I walked out to my car—not brighter, perhaps, but warmer. It washed over me, and over the side of her house, and through the panes of her window, and onto each of the houses up and down Masonic Street, with the same sureness and caring, the same rinsing away of disapproval. And up along the coast that afternoon, driving home, I half imagined I could see it sparkling, farther than the eye could see, on the waves that traveled the Atlantic toward the past and future of the world.

"HERE COMES THE ONLY MAN"

□

One thinks of him as a rebel: E. E. Cummings, the poet who wrote of himself as lower-case *i,* scattered punctuation like spilled pepper across the page, unhinged his sentences and shattered his words, and generally set about to appall his contemporaries.

And so he was a rebel, not only in style but in substance. A sharp-tongued satirist, he pilloried the foibles of his age in words so crisp that they caused the polite to gasp and the worldly to guffaw. He had no patience with hypocrisy and no tolerance for drabness: life, to him, was a thing both honest and bright, and he shot off his barbs wherever he saw counterfeits of these qualities. Sometimes tart, sometimes crude, he was often profound and rarely cowardly. If he erred, it was when his feelings ran helter-skelter, out of earshot of his reason. Even that, however, did not happen by accident: for, as he said in one of his poems, "feeling is first."

Yet behind the pungency, undergirding the feeling,

were two things often missed by those readers who fancy all artists to be nothing but seething pots of emotion. One was his intelligence. Like most comedians (and he was, essentially, a comic writer) he brought to his observations of the world a tremendous insight and an almost scholarly fascination with language. The other was his sense of great affection. Not only did he write some of the twentieth century's most genuine lyric poetry—no easy task in an age bent on self-analysis and shelled over with cynicism. He also had, behind his reclusive behavior, a great sense of love for what redeemed humanity could become.

His poetry, in many ways, is the chart of his search for a redeemer—for something that would save a world made ugly by the two world wars through which he lived, and made sordid by the materialism that spawned them. In his early years he sought salvation in love poetry. As he progressed he came to seek it more and more in a sense of deity, in a supreme source of goodness that appears in his poetry as everything from a vague notion of nature's beneficence to a vision of something very like the Christian's God.

The poem reproduced here is one of the great way-marks of his search. It stands toward the mature end of his career, in a book of poems from 1950 titled "XAIRE"— a Greek word meaning "rejoice" or "greetings," pronounced (as he wrote to an inquirer) "KAI(as in Kaiser) rea(as in ready)." It is a parable; and, true to its genre, it is as expansive of meaning as the reader will let it be.

On its surface, it is a tale of a tinker, an itinerant "mender/ of things" (as he elsewhere called the figure of the scissorsgrinder) who was once a common sight

who sharpens every dull

who sharpens every dull
here comes the only man
reminding with his bell
to disappear a sun

and out of houses pour
maids mothers widows wives
bringing this visitor
their very oldest lives

one pays him with a smile
another with a tear
some cannot pay at all
he never seems to care

he sharpens is to am
he sharpens say to sing
you'd almost cut your thumb
so right he sharpens wrong

and when their lives are keen
he throws the world a kiss
and slings his wheel upon
his back and off he goes

but we can hear him still
if now our sun is gone
reminding with his bell
to reappear a moon

E. E. Cummings

From *Complete Poems: 1913–1962*, by
E. E. Cummings. New York: Harcourt Brace
Jovanovich. 1972.

on city streets. Like the clowns and bums Cummings loved, the tinker lives on the periphery of society, an apparently homeless wanderer who is at home everywhere. But this poem is only partly about the tinker. For the figure here is that of "the only man," the redeemer who "sharpens every dull" and hones the "very oldest lives." Significantly, the word *knives* is missing here: for although both the subject and the rhyme make us think of it, this is a poem about the larger topic, "lives."

And what, exactly, is the nature of his redemptive act? It is primarily verbal—a cleansing of life through a revitalization of language. Sharpening "is to am," he files the general, impersonal sense of the verb into the specific relevance of the first person; sharpening "say to sing," he elevates the merely prosaic to the truly melodic.

Nor is his work mere craftsmanship divorced from deeper meanings. The salvation he brings depends on truth, as he sharpens wrong into right. He has come not for money, nor fame, nor personal satisfaction. His purpose: to make lives "keen," a word Cummings would have known to mean *nifty* or *wonderful* as well as *sharp*. Nor does this redeemer leave us where he found us.

For "if our sun is gone"—if, in Cummings's symbolism, we have overcome the harshness of daylight and mere human reasoning—we will continue to hear his bell, reminding us to seek the more gentle and poetic moonlight.

Who, then, is this "only man"? Is he the Christian Messiah, cast in street garb like a figure out of *Godspell*? Is he the poet, who remakes the world by recasting its language? Or is he "only" a man, nothing more? Whoever he is, he has come to teach us many things: that wrong is only a blunted sense of right, that dullness itself can be healed, and that they who listen (how fitting that they are all female, like the women at the cross in the gospels) are they who will hear the bell, come out of their protective houses, and willingly bring whatever most needs honing. This honing of dull things is full of hope. It is a regeneration far indeed from the condemnation of an earlier poem, which ended "the godless are the dull and the dull are the damned."

And as for the old canard ("But is it poetry?"), one need only read the pulse of its meter and sound the chiming of its near-rhyme ("dull" and "bell," for example) to satisfy the thirst for conventional prosody. But there is more here than mechanics. The poetry lies in the message. The poem sounds a chord as old as literature itself, telling of the mysterious stranger who comes, works his healing miracles, and departs. And it talks, in the end, about literature. For it is a poem about the way words work—about the process whereby human communication, grown faded and wan in the sunlight of mere logic, is refreshed by the reflected light of intuition and feeling. It is also a kind of self-portraiture—a poem about light, done by a man who, though few realized it, spent more time painting than writing.

Ultimately, it is the work of a poet "reminding with his bell" that we, too, in our very oldest lives and language, can be renewed. These days, there are few finer things for a poet to say.

MASTERPAINT
THEATER

☐

"It's supposed to be nice this weekend," my wife said the other day. She's not usually given to meteorological observation. I waited to see what was coming.

"We should probably paint the front porch."

She made it sound easy—the way you might say,"We ought to run downtown for the paper." Our house, however, has what can only be described as a generic Maine front porch—as wide as the building itself, deep enough to store two canoes side by side, and glassed all around with fifteen large, two-paned, wooden-framed windows.

There was no getting around it: she was right. The inside was merely drab, the way paint gets after years of dust and cobwebs. But the outside was on the way to becoming a disgrace. The once-white trim was grayed with age—peeling and flaked where the afternoon sun baked it, and weathered down to unprotected wood where the snow had lodged all winter along the window-ledges. Such putty as had survived lay cracked and rutted, curling away from the glass in rock-hard strips or clinging in corners with chisel-confounding malice. The screens looked as though they had last seen whitewash during the Depression, and one of the panes was broken.

So with the Saturday dew still on the lilacs, I got out paint and brushes—and the putty knife, the assorted bits of sandpaper, the paint scrapers (two), the straight-edged razor blades (left over from wallpapering), four screwdrivers (just in case), the hammer (to add persuasion to the screwdrivers), and two ladders (for effect). Marshaling them in the front yard, I settled down for that solitary, long-distance sail that house painting always becomes.

As it happens, I rather enjoy painting. It's a bit like driving: it demands enough concentration to forestall deep logic but leaves enough space to let the mind wander among its intuitions. But I did begin to wonder whether the generic Maine porch wasn't perhaps an idea whose time had come and gone. We had a private deck out the back. Would we really get much use from this public one? Besides, it was a beautifully cool, sunny day: For all that I was content to be outdoors, I felt slightly trapped, cut off from the wakening bustle of a small-town Saturday.

"Looking good!"

I squinted toward the sidewalk at the familiar voice. They had paused on their walk downtown, the couple and their children from a few doors up the hill. Any port in a storm, I thought, climbing down to chat for a moment on the edge of the lawn. They were on their way to breakfast out, and we talked about the virtues of hired painters until the children, hot on the scent of cinnamon buns, tugged irresistibly on the leash of parental responsibility. I went back to the irresponsible putty.

Before long I heard a car idling in the street. "You're working pretty hard, stranger," called the passenger. She'd just returned, along with her husband, from the South for the summer; my wife had helped them pack up last fall, my daughter had agreed to babysit for the one thing they dared not put in storage, a sprawling black teddy bear about the size of Monhegan Island. The three of us chatted in the sunlight about the virtues of maintenance-free dwellings until we felt embarrassed at how much work I wasn't getting done.

By noon the project was developing a certain rhythm—and I was beginning to notice that working on a generic Maine porch was hardly solitary. The dogs came in and out. Several folks I hardly knew waved and spoke as they walked past. A friend returned some sheets she had borrowed for a surge of weekend houseguests. My daughter's friends came by, chatting amicably as they hopped over the tools and went inside. A neighbor offered his power sander; several pickup trucks honked on their way to the dump; a couple I hadn't seen since a late-evening dog-walk after the last blizzard paused as they were strolling home.

And that, I thought as I cleaned up the tools, is what front porches are all about. I'd always thought of them as places to sit "of an evening" and watch the world pass by. They are. But they're something more. They're places to be seen.

To our privacy-craving age that sounds strange, almost immodest. Yet that's what builds a sense of community—that willingness not only to see but to be seen. Too often, trapped in our busy shells of aloofness, we think of front porches only as places where the nosy keep their unsleeping vigil over a world of gossip. Sometimes they are. But they're also for those who, by the very act of sitting there so publicly, invite conversation with the passersby—who as much as say, "I'm not thinking anything that can't wait: Come share a thought."

And what are communities, after all, but sets of shared thoughts. Man cannot live—not, at least, in small-town Maine—by back porches alone.

FRUSTRATION
AND THE
FRENCH HORN

□

In the world of music, there may be no sadder sight than that of a small boy with a large French horn.

I know: I was one.

It was at the tender age of ten that I came under the spell of that slippery and mysterious piece of tubing; and for the next three years, until I retreated into the relative safety of the trombone, my musical life was one *ostinato* of frustration. Please don't misunderstand: I still think the French horn is one of the most lyrical and lovely of instruments—when it is played right. It is just that I was very clearly not the right player.

I suppose the thing got off on the wrong note at the very outset. Like any red-blooded American boy, I wanted to play the trumpet. So, of course, did all the other boys. And as a thirty-piece band with nineteen trumpeters is, to say the least, a bit lopsided, the director very wisely urged us toward diversification. To the stout he extolled the virtues of the tuba. To the more wiry and active, he declared his fondness for clarinets and saxophones. The violent and mischievous found release among the drums. And for the shy, earnest types—of which, I think, I was one—were reserved such beautiful and exacting instruments as French horns and oboes.

Now, I've never played an oboe. But I'm told it is difficult, simply because it demands such restraint. The player, like a kind of human bagpipe, puffs himself full of wind, squeezes it to tremendous pressure, and then lets it leak out in a long, agonizing trickle. Bad enough, I'm sure. But at least—oh, how I envied them!—the oboists whose fingers pressed the proper keys got the notes they wanted. It was really that simple: learn to blow, master the fingering, *et voila!*—there was the note.

With the French horn it is quite otherwise. Nothing is easier than to make a noise: purse your lips, blast away into the mouthpiece, and out comes a sound. Nor does the problem lie in the fingering. It has but three valves, and any beginner's book will tell you which combinations correspond to which note. So there you are—if you believe everything you read. In fact, as I soon found out, the fingering chart is a mere tissue of prevarication, an artifice promising certainty and delivering nothing but mystery. For so long is the instrument's air column, and so numerous are the possible notes that each fingering can produce, that the novice is instantly adrift on a kind of black night of the scale. Press the valves, blow, and any one of seven notes comes forth. Which one, it seemed to me, was wholly a matter of chance.

The problem was particularly acute at entrances. Once you got well and truly launched into a line of notes, you could estimate how large a leap it would take to reach the next note. In itself, that fact never ensured accuracy, but at least you could tell (after the fact) whether the shot was too high or too low. But at entrances there was nothing to guide you. Not only could you be egregiously mistaken, you could easily go blithely on without even *realizing* you were mistaken.

Worse still, the French horn parts we got were full of long rests. So there were plenty of entrances. There you sat, with this great coil of plumbing gradually growing cold in your lap, trying not to lose count as the measures passed. Suddenly it appeared: your high F-sharp, standing out unprotected like a lone tree on a high plain. To this day I squirm when I hear horn players making an entrance in even the finest symphonies. All but the best of them remind me of nearsighted burglars, bungling at least half their attempts to break into the score. How they must envy the oboists.

Back in those days, however, it was not the orchestra but the marching band that ultimately undid me. Nobody, designing either a marching band or a French horn in an ideal world, would dream of putting one with the other. There you were, stumbling about with your hand wedged awkwardly up the bell, trying to keep your lips firmly on the tiny mouthpiece that bobbed like a cork on the tide. I suspect the arrangers who scored the marches included horns only out of misplaced sympathy. Every band, they must have reasoned, would have a few unfortunates condemned to play the thing, so it was only fair to give them a part. But the best they could think to give us was a series of offbeats. So we scuffed around the playground in our white bucks and blazers; and while all the good tunes went to the trumpets and trombones, we played one-*poot*-one-*poot* from start to finish.

Well, I stuck it out as long as I could. I even bought my own horn, an ancient silver-colored apparatus with an E-flat attachment that made it look like the insides of somebody's boiler. But one day, nosing about alone in the band-room storage closet after school, I came upon a trombone. No one had checked it out. Tentatively, hesitantly, I opened it and put it together. I studied its large, stable-looking mouthpiece. I gave the slide a few preliminary thrusts. Then, looking about—it seemed almost disloyal—I put it to my lips and blew. Out came a sound—it was so simple, so pure. I moved the slide. Obediently, the note changed.

Quietly, I put it back, shut the case, filled out a loan card, and took it home. The rest is history. Well, personal history.

LOCKING
IN
BEAUTY

☐

I almost threw it away. Like the others, it was so layered with paint that it revealed its shape—that of a window-lock—only in the most general ways. I had unscrewed it from its ledge where the two sashes meet in order to paint the windows. Fiddling with it, I noticed its spring was broken. One more item in this old house of ours, I thought, needing replacement. No matter: a nuisance, perhaps, but of little value. The new ones would probably be better.

So it lay in an old pie plate while winter shaded into spring and the painting got done. And then, a few weeks ago, it happened into the batch of other fixtures to be cleaned up. Feeling genial and inclusive—for one cannot venture into paint removal unless time would otherwise hang heavy—I let it take its place among the batch.

Now, there is a certain thrill of discovery attendant upon renovation. Some discoveries are small, like noticing the square nail in the stairwell. Some are large, like finding hand-hewn beams under the living room ceiling. And some, small in size, are large in significance.

Like the window-lock. The paint remover took it gradually back through the strata of its history, from white to light green and down to a particularly astonishing red. And as I chipped and scraped, one thing became most apparent. This was no ordinary window-lock.

It was, in fact, a minor piece of art, or, if that term needs to be reserved for special use, of artisanship. Steel most of the way, it culminated in a brass handle on the top. But what left me staring was the detail. Both base and brass were laced with a frieze of decoration around the edge, the intricate lines founded in low relief.

What could they have had in mind, I remember thinking—those old boys who lavished such care on an ordinary window-lock? Were they casting about for extra work? Were they laboring at the cutting edge of high fashion? Were they trembling under the watchful eye of buyers who would toss aside their work if it were less than the hardware equivalent of *haute couture*? Or were they responding to the demands of the Edwardian age (from which I suppose it came) and compelling even the most indifferent items to combine beauty with utility?

Grabbing a rag, I wiped it dry and ran to show my wife—for all the world, no doubt, like a five-year-old with a new toy bulldozer. But what else does one do in those situations? Some things have to be shared— although I suspect her kindly expression of interest was tempered with surprise that such trivia could generate such delight. But there it was, and I was no more free to set it aside unheralded than a returning Columbus would have been able to reply to Queen Isabella's question "What did you find?" with "Oh, nothing."

But what had I found, anyway? Surely it was more than a broken bit of metal. And surely it was more than the satisfaction of having staved off costly repair with thrift.

In the end, I suppose, my delight had something to do with coming back in touch, however fleetingly, with a lost age. It was as though, in a small and delicate way, I had discovered an entire ethic. For I strongly suspect that, in ages as in individuals, our largest motives and concerns are in fact revealed in our approach to the smallest things. I remember once reading an essay by an art connoisseur who was convinced that he could detect forged portraits by looking at the ears. He reasoned that no painter bothered to study his subject's individual ears. Instead, he simply reproduced his own conception of the ear in every painting, in a style as characteristic of him as his own fingerprint. As ears to Michelangelo, so window-locks to fixturemakers: items so insignificant that they allowed unconscious habits to reflect an entire period.

And if so, what were those artisans saying? Maybe only this: that there are ways of living that elevate even the most mundane objects into a place in the pattern of our lives. That every made thing upon which the eye lights has the capacity to satisfy our innate sense of visual design. And that no opportunity for providing that satisfaction, however tiny, ought to be lost.

It is a cast of mind that, as words like *productivity* and *cost* rise in popularity, we seem to be losing. And yet, I furtively wonder, *is* that a loss entirely to be regretted? For living among tradition is so often confused, these days, with living among decoration—filling one's home, or town, or country, with so many items from the past that the new has little chance to take root. Even a window-lock has a responsibility to bear in that milieu. Maybe, after all, an unobtrusive, undecorated lock is an admission of great humility. Maybe it confesses that the natural world beyond the window, rather than anything man might set in its way, is what most matters.

Yet even there, so close upon a conclusion, comes the eternal "but." For what if our modern locks are no more than expressions of carelessness? What if all they mean is, "Here is something stamped out with no imagination and got on the cheap"? What will they say, those tinny ear-shaped things, about us to future ages?

I don't know. I've refitted the unpainted lock to the window again and put back the tools. No doubt some future craftsman, seized by the desire for consistency, will paint it woodwork-color again. And so it will go, posing its question over and over, carrying forward that potential for discovery which elevates life out of drabness into grace.

THE
TOOL *JUSTE*

□

M y dear,

Looking back, I can see I should have allowed more time. A one-minute break at a high school basketball game in a small Maine town, after all, doesn't lend itself to much depth. But somehow it needed saying.

You may remember, as we leaned back against the varnished-wood bleachers, that I said casually, "I finally bought myself something I've always wanted."

"Mm," you said, gazing across the gym floor at the huddle of undifferentiated players, "What was it?"

"A plug wrench," I replied.

You turned, giving me that wonderfully quizzical look. "You've always wanted a *plug wrench?*" it seemed to say. "How come you never told me? And why did you buy it *now,* just before Christmas, when our children are racking their brains trying to think of gifts for you? Can I really have married a man whose idea of a good time is buying a plug wrench? I thought I was married to a writer. Are you being serious?"

In fact, all you said was, "What on earth's a plug wrench?"

"A socket wrench for changing spark plugs in the car," I explained. "Long and deep, so it fits over the plug—otherwise there's no way to get 'em out. Funny kind of tool: you can't really use it for anything else, but when you need it, nothing else will do."

"Oh," you said as the buzzer sounded and the teams sauntered out, stirring up faint odors of rubber and popcorn and perspiration. Then you patted my hand in mock overconcern. "That's nice," you said with a gentle laugh.

Our boys won, and we got talking about other things, and the matter dropped. And I never really explained what being a writer and owning a plug wrench have in common. So let me try.

That morning, the National Weather Service had nailed it perfectly. "Bitter cold," said the voice on the radio, and it was right. I layered up and went to check the cars, thinking about the language of forecasts. *Bitter,* I'd been told, was actually a technical term for the weather service, the third leg down in a range that went from *cold* and *very cold* through *bitter cold* to *extreme cold.* Up in these parts, *wicked* would also fit pretty well. So would *awful, mis'rable,* or *pretty dahn.* But *bitter* was the precisely accurate tool, designed to do one job alone. The others were more doubtful.

So was my car, which turned over grudgingly and refused to start. "It's the wind," said Glen when, twenty minutes after I'd called, he showed up in the John's Gulf truck and backed into the driveway. "I got 'bout twenty calls like this this morning," he added cheerfully. He clipped on the jumper cables and cranked over the engine. Still no response. He'd put me on the list for the tow truck, he said as he left.

And that's when I noticed the loose spark plug. There was fuel leaking out around its base. Pulling off the wire, I found I could unscrew it with my fingers. Something, obviously, wasn't right. It was covered with black gunk.

"What the heck's *that*?!" said the fellow at the auto-parts place in genuine amazement when, a few minutes later, I laid it on the counter.

"It was loose," I replied. "I need a new set of plugs."

"Well I guess!" he said, thumbing through a catalog.

"Better have a plug wrench, too," I added when he returned from the back room with four new plugs.

The whole thing pretty much chewed up a twenty. "Don't tighten 'em down too much, now," he said as I left. "Be the devil to pay next time you gotta change 'em."

I remember thinking that was good advice. I also recall wondering how he knew I didn't know that already. When I thought about it, of course, the answer was obvious. It wasn't that I didn't have grease under my nails or that I talked like someone from away. It was that, until that very moment, I didn't own a plug wrench.

Now, you can go a long way in life with just a screw-driver and a pair of pliers. But you can't be serious about cars without a more refined set of tools. In fact, you can measure that seriousness, that maturity, by the kind of tools you own. The more tools you buy, the more you find they resemble one another—almost identical on the outside, hiding their peculiar strains of usefulness within. If you care about tools, you come to relish those shades of gray.

Which is true with words, too. It's in the subtle distinctions, not the broad swaths, that works of great precision get done. In the end, that's also where individuality resides. I guess that's what I would have said to you that night at the game—that, in some small way, maturity and individuality arise from differentiation. You go through the years building up a vocabulary—just as you build up a tool collection. It gets stocked with fancy words and thunderous phrases—and with plain, accurate, kitchen-variety terms. And for what? Sometimes for great occasions. And sometimes just to deal with the weather. But always so that, when the time comes, the tool fits the job.

With great affection.

MARBLES
ON A
WINDOW
LEDGE

□

T hat fall, the trees along Kellogg Avenue shed leaves like shreds of brown arithmetic paper. They floated past the windows of Miss Powers's third-grade classroom, swirling across the new-paved playground where the janitor had painted basketball courts and the girls had chalked their hop-scotch. Eventually they lodged against the low wire fence in the corner where the shade was thick and the brown earth packed and grassless.

I never knew whether Miss Powers had been drawn to teaching by her name or had taken the name after she entered her first classroom. Whichever way, it was a perfect match—especially with the "s." She was a woman of many parts, but without a despotic bone in her body. Strong-handed but happy-voiced, youthful but firm, she kept us in enough order to learn—with enough humor to relax. Under her watchful eye and pretty face, it somehow mattered that if Jenny traded fourteen gumballs to Suzy for four cookies, each cookie was worth three-and-a-half gumballs. It was all a perfectly natural part of a morning's work.

But so, of course, were the bells at recess-time. If we had been bad—for even the best of us had to be forever probing the limits of teacherly patience—the bell meant a session of washing blackboards, clapping erasers on the fire-escape, or writing "I will never again pass notes to Ann" fifty times on white composition paper. But on normal days the bell was still ringing as Charlie and Tut and Dave and Steve and the rest of us thundered down the stairs for twenty minutes of glorious irresponsibility.

And for marbles. Once outside, we would make for that corner where the leaves gathered. Brushing them aside with a foot, we would kick in the ground a heel-deep hole as big around as a baseball. Several paces away we would draw the foul line. And then we would take out our marbles.

Where they came from I was never sure. I have no recollection of ever buying any—although Hastings's had them for sale at the back of the store with the squirt guns and the model airplane kits, in little net sacks with stapled paper labels. Now and then you found them under bushes or in the street gutters on the way home. But mostly you just had them. Years later, I heard the tale of the young wife who asked a prominent Boston dowager where she got her wonderful hats. "My dear," the lady replied haughtily. "we don't *get* our hats—we *have* our hats." I guess that was the way of it about our marbles.

Except, of course, that you could always win them! To that end we selected carefully, each morning, the marbles we were willing to hazard at that day's recess. Some brought them in string-throated muslin bags or small flip-lidded tobacco tins. But most of us kept them in the pockets of what we called (since the word "jeans" had yet to win its current cachet) our dungarees. We brought them in all varieties: as small as overgrown peas, as large as jaw-breaker gumballs, clear silver and purple and green and red, or porcelain-smooth and opaque with swirls of color. Some had a steel-hued metallic sheen, flecked with brighter spots like stars seen through haze. Others were strangely made cat's-eyes, with ribbons of color set deep inside their transparent globes. I remember collecting thirty-some-odd in a pattern of azure, gray, and white, like a sunset before it turns pink. I even had, once, a stainless-steel ball bearing; but I lost it to Dave, who was reputed to have had one of the largest marble collections in town.

I don't remember exactly how the game was played— except that we chucked our marbles, underhand, from behind the line and then flicked them into the pit with bent forefingers. Somehow it was a winner-take-all affair: I remember feelings of triumph in scooping up and pocketing whole pitfuls, and of remorse as a much-loved challenger vanished into a friend's grasp. Not that prowess at the marble-pitch was the only way to collect. I once got a very fine jackknife in trade for several prize boulders, and dispensed with an unwanted Cub Scout scarf-ring in the same fashion.

It had been years since I'd given a thought to marbles when, on a whim, my wife and I poked into an art museum gift shop in Maine. There, on the counter by the cash register, were great jars full of marbles— transparent primary colors in several sizes, each one shot through with tiny bubbles like an effervescence frozen in mid-flight. I had never seen so many marbles all in one place, and I stood transfixed, forgetting the prints of Homer and Seurat and Hartley in the dazzle of the glass. They could be had, said the sign, for fifteen cents apiece. For the longest time I hung back. Then, rather sheepishly, looking round to be sure my wife wasn't watching, I bought a small bagful and squirrelled them away quickly in my pocket.

Why, I thought as we were driving home, was buying marbles such an odd thing to do? Why had I hesitated so long—and why, when I bought them, did it leave me with such a strange feeling? I'm not much of a shopper, I thought—happy to buy gifts for others, but unwilling to buy something only for myself. But that wasn't it, exactly. Nor, I realized, was it simply that I couldn't think what to do with the marbles once I had them. I've bought my share of old church-fair books I never open, odd-shaped mugs I never drink from, and antique tools that rust in the cellar. A few marbles would hardly matter. Nor, surely, was I daunted by the price. I still have the receipt: "$1.74," it says. "Thank you very much."

We drove on and came to a place where the lush open fields roll right up to the road, breaking across its slender shoal and washing past to the far woods. As we passed a "for sale" sign, it hit me: It was like buying money. Marbles, I realized, were not things you *bought,* because they had always been themselves the counters of wealth, the setters of worth, the coinage with which one purchased other things. Seeing them for sale was like seeing a pile of nickels on the counter with a card saying, "five cents each." It was as though I had stumbled into a mint and found the coin of the realm fresh-made and waiting to be circulated and valued.

Yet even our coins have behind them an age-old urge for beauty—a sense of design, of letter and line, of weight and balance. And so it was, I suddenly realized, with our marbles. Value? Yes, they had that, with all the precision that a school-boy economy could establish. But beyond that they were, in their own way and in our new-minted world, works of art. Miss Powers never taught us the word "aesthetics," and we would have thought it sissy to use it if she had. But there was more than just value going on when, sizing up the marbles in hand compared to those offered in trade, we would hesitate for minutes on end, shifting from foot to foot and staring, helpless to define a sense of attachment to a beauty we hardly knew we felt.

That was years ago. I guess I still don't know how we establish value—how we set the worth of rare things against the value of the commonplace. But in some coins, and in the marbles of my youth, beauty and a medium of exchange are married. Only in the "adult" world, I guess, is a crumpled dollar bill worth more than the sunlight shining through those marbles on a window ledge.

IN THE
BACKYARDS
OF OUR
LIVES

□

It was a white frame Victorian affair, the house I grew up in, standing on its own acre in the small college town of Amherst, Massachusetts. It dated from the 1850s—an imposing two-story cube with a kind of mortarboard roof, three-chimneyed, black-shuttered, broad-eaved. It had been built by a prosperous farmer on what was originally quite a large tract. He cared less for display than structure: although the house was well enough appointed, embellished here and there with fancy molding or mantelpiece or cornice, it sported none of the gingerbread gaucherie marring its neighbors. It was on the unseen that this Yankee lavished his care, sinking a cellar of stones only oxen could have moved, framing his structure out of studs twice the size of those that pass, nowadays, for two-by-fours. He seemed to have built it, strangely enough, from clear lumber: in all our cuttings and alterings we never uncovered a single knot. What we did uncover was a full layer of brick under the outerwalls of the first story, as though he had secreted something of himself deep within the walls.

By the time our family arrived, so had the railroad. It ran along the hillside behind the houses, which, looking out onto Main Street, piously shunned its existence, turning to it the backsides in their disdain. Our acre screened off the tracks behind a bunch of elms we called The Woods. Naturally it was to The Woods, rather than Main Street, that we children turned our playtime energies; and so we grew rather fond of the railroad. We learned to adapt our paces to the devilishly inconvenient distance between railroad ties, taking them giantly two at a time or mincing along one by one, coolie-fashion. We learned to walk all the way to Strong Street along a single rail.

We never worried about the trains. They came with a pleasant infrequency, carrying nothing but freight up into Vermont. They were drawn by steam locomotives, black and bulging things that wore all their machinery and tubes and valves on the outsides of their boilers. The engines would stop for water at a tank tower near the woods and then sit hissing and chuffing by the nearby crossing, waiting for some inscrutable event to occur down the line before they could wheeze themselves to life and be off. Often, at night, they would send their steam-blown, reedy cries through the elm tops into my room, then pound past the house, rattling the double-hung sashes in their casements.

But progress also pounded past, and we put up storm windows and took the coal grates out of our fireplaces; and the line changed to diesel engines, and people took to traveling by car and airplane. So it wasn't until last year that I rode for any real distance on a train, clicketing back from New York through rural Connecticut toward the town of my boyhood.

I sat that day looking through the dirty window at the landscape. The railway bed resembled the one behind our house—crushed rock blackened by the nearness of oily machinery. Then the steep embankment, tumbling down into alders and pussy willows and the furred, anonymous shrubs of New England back corners. Then a swampish brook, a rusted-out truck or two, and beyond a stretch of hummocky land climbing painfully but steadily into open fields. And across the fields, near or far as the scene changed, the weathered ends of barns and chicken coops, the backs of houses, the casual litter of country living. Here and there, a group of children standing aside, waiting for us to get off their rails. Here and there, a forgotten dump, rotting washing-machines and bedsprings; and once, off on a sidetrack, a great dangling growth of poles and wires and huge lion's-mane brushes that had been meant to wash railroad cars. Unkempt, useless, it was overgrown with wild blackberries.

This landscape, I thought to myself, has all the elements of ugliness. Yet it's not exactly ugly. There is, in all this sprawled welter of discardings, something appealing, even moving. What is it? I've thought of it since—especially in driving along on winding country highways. There, the undersides of things are kept safely at bay: houses face the road, putting their best front forward. Our roads, after all, show us the public faces of our society, the faces we prepare, as the poet T. S. Eliot once said, to meet the faces that we meet. Railroads show us something else: nobody turns his good side to the tracks. The privacies of things, the intimate mingled with the seedy, the tacky and personal all intermixed: that's the railroad view. Why should that odd mix be so appealing?

Recently, rereading Joseph Conrad's *Heart of Darkness,* I came upon an answer. Marlow the storyteller begins with the words, " 'I don't want to bother you much with what happened to me personally.' " To which Conrad the narrator objects, noting that Marlow's remark shows "the weakness of many tellers of tales who seem so often unaware of what their audience would best like to hear." Conrad is right: what catches the fancy is less the mind that abstracts than the eye that details, not the impersonal grandeur of love and beauty, but the "I" capable of noticing the torn pocket on the overalls hung out in the dooryard to dry. What moves us in fiction—and in life—is not the public faces but the private intimacies, not the ways we deport ourselves while being watched, but the ways we frolic or lounge when we're most ourselves.

That's true of houses, too. The facades, the halls, the living rooms—these tell us of a world that ought to be. But the attics and pantries, the cobwebs in the woodshed window, the china left by children under the spruce—these testify to so much more, to the personal curve of life as it is actually led. The passerby on the highway sees only the grand and decorous. It is left to the faces at the Pullman windows, and to children walking the rails, to find us out in all the private backyards of our lives.

O RARE
MISS DONLEY

☐

To us, she was Miss Donley. She rode our high school Latin classroom as an equestrian rides a spirited horse: patiently, but thoughtfully, with unequivocal firmness. Perhaps the firmness was a good thing, for as students we were, if not exactly wild, certainly more given to action than serenity. Only outside her pillared and charioted bulletin boards would we play our little pranks, slamming lockers in gladiatorial bravado and swaggering as only a sophomore among seniors can swagger. Once having entered her precincts (so stark and austere after the stuffed luxuries of the biology lab down the hall), we came under the spell of her polished blackboards. There, our studied disregard for learning having given way to a grudging fascination, we sang of nouns and the man, groped among the irregular verbs, and were invariably ambushed by the ablative absolute.

There, too, we believed that all knowledge, like all Gaul, is divided into three parts: the practical, the theoretical, and the esoteric. The first was nicely exemplified in our English class, where we studied a book whose title (*Thirty Days to a More Powerful Vocabulary*) sounded rather like a cross between a self-help tract and a jail sentence. The second, the theoretical, was the province of geometry, where I recall that we once debated the possibility that zero was infinity. The esoteric was clearly embodied in the Roman tongue: ornate, convoluted, full of fine sounds, and entirely useless.

Or so we thought. For which of us, puzzling piecemeal through Caesar's exploits, could recognize the value of such an immersion in antiquity? In those true-false days, the fact was king. He who was smartest had the head most full of useful detail. We came to *The Gallic War* as to algebraic equations, intent on "solving" it into English. Never mind that it told us of a wholly different age and conscience; never mind that around the edges of the words glimmered the penumbra of a strange new world of feeling. Feelings couldn't be memorized or graded. In the press toward facts, feelings remained on the horizon. Despite our appetite for such facts, Miss Donley reined us in and headed us toward that distant world.

How thoroughly our priorities were disordered never occurred to me until much later. I remember, in college, getting into a silly squabble with a fellow student about the dative case. His Latin, it seems, was better than mine, and so of course he won. But what astonished me was how little I remembered from my studies. I could still smell the classroom. And I had a clear sense for the sound of the steeds in the night, the watchfires signaling from hill to hill, and the breastplated centurion sweeping back the flap of his tent as the mist lifted over what we now call France. The feelings remained. But I knew nothing of the dative case.

There, perhaps, lies the real reason behind the study of language: to learn how to feel. Our poets have been telling us that for centuries, you say? Just so—and yet we go right on believing that learning a new language is no more than a matter of memorizing some one-to-one correspondences. *Snow,* we say, imagining that it translates into the Latin *nix, nivis*. But what it means to me, sitting before my fire on a New England winter's evening, bears little relation to what it must have meant to a Roman soldier, child of Mediterranean sunlight, as he stood guard along Hadrian's Wall in the north of England in a swirling blizzard of *nix*.

If I were inclined to jeremiads—or even if I simply wanted to run severe storm warnings up the flagpole of twentieth-century civilization—I would decry the loss of the study of foreign tongues. Not for all the official reasons—that it opens international understanding, that it teaches etymology, that it disciplines the memory, or even that it is in high demand among diplomats and import-export traders. No, I would see in its waning a sign of a loss of sensibility, an atrophy of our already tenuous capacity to *feel*. So much of that capacity, I think, relates to our use of language. How better to shift into new feelings, then, than by shifting tongues?

If I were looking for another renaissance—another transformation as great as that which culminated in the Elizabethan age—I would seek it not among men of facts, nor among computers talking one to another, nor in a society which speaks, as ours does, progressively in

81

numbers. I would seek it among those who are willing to let language convey to them not only an *understanding of* but a *feeling for* one another. I would look for it less among those who say, "I must know what this Roman thought," than among those who say, "I must sense what this Roman felt."

And for you, O rare Miss Donley, I would invent a new past tense, a kind of perfect imperative. With it I would say: "Have taught me Latin well enough that I can afford to forget its details. Have brought me through the thickets of grammar into the open leas of feeling. Have raised my awareness of all that lies beyond reason. Have shown me poetry where, in my ignorance, I thought there were only words."

HAWK'S NEST

☐

"Tomorrow," said my sister, "we'll go to Hawk's Nest."

It was, for a seven-year-old, the dream of a lifetime. She was twice my age; and for years, it seemed, I had heard about Hawk's Nest. Not that I was sure just what it was. I knew only that it was way out in the woods, and had to do with a river and some sand. I knew that it was a long walk from our house, and that it was positively the most wonderful place you could imagine. I knew that its name was shrouded in mystery—that it had nothing to do with either hawks or nests. And, of course, I knew that it was "secret"—a word which, more than any amount of mere description, assured me of its desirability.

I had come of age to share the secret. So I was feeling particularly grown up when we set out early, lunch bags in hand, into the fine June morning. We followed the railroad tracks for the first mile, then turned down Strong Street, cut through the woods, and came to a field. Some distance away stood a farmhouse.

"Shh!" said my sister, holding open the strands of barbed wire for me to climb through. "Crouch down!"

Stooping over, Indian-fashion, she ran across the crest of the hill and disappeared through the far fence. I followed, obediently bent double—though I recall wondering why. The farmhouse commanded a full view of us however we went.

But our game seemed to work. No one yelled at us, and pretty soon we were walking briskly along North East Street, our jackets tied around our waists, talking of this and that. On our left were more fields. On the right, cow pastures sloped gently down to a border of trees a long ways back. Beyond them, faintly blue in the distance, rose the Pelham Hills.

After a while my sister slowed the pace, looked furtively around—though by now the nearest house was almost out of hailing—and suddenly darted into a narrow dirt road on the right. I followed. The track ran flat beside pines, planted some years back in rows, and finally emerged in a kind of gravelly turnaround.

"The rifle range," she whispered, pointing ahead of us.

I could see nothing but trees. But she soon found a sandy path running through the slowly warming underbrush. We were coming up over a little rise when she grabbed my arm. There, two steps ahead, the brush stopped abruptly at a ten-foot ditch. It was lined with concrete. Looking over the edge, I saw great rusted contraptions of gears and levers.

"For targets," she said. "From the war. See?"

She plucked a spent cartridge from the sand and handed it to me. I was astonished. I knew vaguely about the war, knew that my best friend's dad kept a brown

Army hat on the top of a glass-doored cupboard in his living room. And as a boy whose backyard often doubled as the Wild West, I knew a Colt from a Winchester. But here was a touch of the real thing. Here was a place in which the imagination could run wild. Here we could play for hours with pine-branch rifles, taking trench after trench from fierce enemies battling among the old machinery.

"So this is Hawk's Nest," I breathed.

My sister paused, then laughed.

"No, dummy, this is the rifle range. Hawk's Nest is over here."

More scrub. More barbed wire. A marshy meadow, the mid-morning sun by now hot and strong, and wet shoes. Then a strangely open forest, with no underbrush but with odd sweeps of gravel and logs scattered about where the river, in its spring flood, had put them. And finally the river itself—a wide stream, really, gurgling over glossy red-brown stones.

We followed it downstream for a ways, and came around a bend. My sister stopped.

"There it is," she said.

I found myself looking at a wide, vast bank of sand on the far side of the river—more sand than I had ever seen. Its toes stood in the water, from which it angled steeply upward. And far above, higher than a steeple of a church, was its head, a vertical wall of hard sand overhung with a thatch of sod like the forelock of a giant. Growing from its top were the ever-present pines.

I have never been able to explain why, in the hours that followed, I was so awed. I had seen a lot of sand before. I had eaten lunches in the woods. I had even stripped to my underwear and plunged into streams before, coming out screaming to dance and shiver on a fallen tree trunk until the sun and my motion dried me.

Nor was it simply the exhilaration of our antics in the sand. We would race each other, orangutan-like, to the top, using hands and feet to scramble through the soft and sliding sand. In the shadow of the top wall, beneath the cliff swallows' holes, we rested, looking down on the treetops across the sun-sparkled stream. Then suddenly we would spring outward in tremendous kangaroo leaps, bounding in great arcs down the slope to the river. Up and down we went, over and over, until the afternoon sun wore away and we had to leave for home.

No, it was not simply my newness to the place that created its special aura. In the years that followed, I returned many times, and the specialness never waned. Part of it, no doubt, was in its remoteness. Had it been closer, or accessible by car, it would have lost that feeling of a goal hard won. And part of it was the sense of responsibility demanded by that very distance—the grownup seriousness of spending a whole day away from home.

But as I think back on it, I see that the true specialness of Hawk's Nest lay in its capacity to be nothing but itself. We never seemed to play at anything there—never pretended it was a mountain full of enemy soldiers, or the river a raging Yukon torrent full of grizzly bears, or the fallen log that bridged it a ship full of buccaneers. It was enough, somehow, that it was Hawk's Nest.

LARRY,
TONY,
AND
"THE TRAIN"

□

At the foot of our street, the bough of a sugar maple shines out in Chinese red. The morning air, these days, is as tart as pie-apples; and the sun, slanting over sidewalks and under hedges, warms the afternoons with the scent of acorns crushed by the feet of schoolchildren. Evenings come early, full of wood smoke and stars, and the nights cycle down to frost.

I suppose, being of a literary bent, that the season ought to remind me of Henry David Thoreau and Robert Frost and the rest of New England's poetic alchemists who have taken autumn and sublimed it into a state of the soul. I *do* think about them, to be sure. But I also think about football.

I'm not much of a sports fan. Now and then I get a kick out of watching part of a televised game. But I don't follow the rankings in the papers, and I would promptly fail any quiz asking for the names of the NFL teams. I never played on high school or college squads.

So why, in this season of sere leaves, should I be reminded of football?

It's because, like most small-town boys in New England, I grew up playing the game. No one ever actually said, "Do you *like* football?" or "Do you want to play?" You played more or less the way you went to the Wednesday night dancing class at the gym—because it was there, because everybody else was doing it, and because it never occurred to you not to.

We started playing, naturally enough, in backyards. I always liked hiking the ball and catching short laterals. But I never got the hang of passing. I suspected the others of secretly spending hours throwing footballs at Coke bottles. Some could launch butter-smooth, perfectly rifled bullets. My passes always wobbled frantically, like a car out of alignment. I remember being greatly relieved when miniature, six-inch footballs became all the rage. Here was something I could get my hands around and send sailing toward the rock garden with the best of them.

The rock garden itself, however, was another story. In those days the fashion in backyard landscaping was to break up every honest expanse of lawn with day lilies, quince bushes, flagstone paths, stands of lilac, rose arbors, and a hundred other hazards all calculated to trip up the unwary. More than once I can recall watching receiver and defender sail high into the air, hang suspended while wrestling each other for the ball, and drop completely out of sight into a shoulder-high stand of flowers. Dreading the parental rebuke whistled smartly from the back porch, we would hastily lean the broken stalks upright against one another and call a couple of safe running plays.

After a while, when it became clear that football and horticulture didn't mix, we took to playing on the long, gently sloping piece of town common near the junior high school. It had a towering elm at one end and a rusting pipe-fence at the other, and it stood next to the woods that led to Emily Dickinson's sister's house. We'd stake out the four corners with windbreakers and lunch boxes and get down to business.

It was there that we discovered, much to everyone's amazement, that at a dead run on the downhill grade I could catch Tut Hewlitt. Nobody could catch Tut Hewlitt—or so it was thought. I think I only did so once or twice. But on those occasions I basked in all the glory that ten-year-olds can bestow, and for a while was among those picked near the top when we chose up sides.

Even then, however, it was apparent that some of that group were destined for higher athletic achievement and that the rest of us, lured into music or drama or hot rods or words, were obviously not. My future in football became unavoidably clear on the day our sixth-grade room played the other room up at the new high school field.

It was a stacked deck from the start. Our teacher, Mrs. Bartlett, was a strictly grammatical and pleasantly indoor type. Try as she would, she had little to say that could inspire us on the playing field. Mr. Edmonds's class, however, seemed to live and breathe football. Besides, they had Larry, Tony, and "the train."

I got to know Larry later—he was the drummer in our band and the soul of gentleness. At that time, however, his importance lay elsewhere. He was huge, fast, and solid as a sledgehammer. Tony, by contrast, was a wire-and-leather farm kid, smaller than I was but wily as a weasel. He could slip out of anybody's grip, and his sneakers fairly steamed as he tore past. And "the train"? It was nothing more than Tony with the ball and Larry out front blocking.

On the afternoon of the big match I was playing defense. We were always playing defense, it seemed, and they were rolling over us like a mowing machine through the rowen. Nor were they very imaginative. Play by play, they just loaded the ball onto the train and sent it pounding through our backfield. I remember my feelings going from astonishment to frustration to rage and finally to fool-hardiness. At last, in a state verging on sheer vengeance, I vowed to do something. The next time the train rounded our line, I wound up like a spring and launched myself directly at Larry.

Even today I can feel the sensation. I ran, as near as I could tell, into the trunk of an oak, bounced gasping into the air, and came thudding to the ground. Larry never even changed his footwork: it was as though he had brushed me off like a barn fly. When I managed to recover my wind and roll over to look, he and Tony were specks on the horizon, greasing across the goal line.

Football was never the same after that. In later years I spent many an hour in the stands—watching, cheering, playing trombone with the band. But I no longer had any desire to be out there on the field. Nor did I ever become, as I say, a "real" sports fan.

But somewhere deep inside, as the seasons change, the old spirit still stirs. So what if I'm not a fan. So what if I don't know the ins and outs of football. That doesn't mean I don't *feel* the game.

WINDOW
SEAT

☐

In the old days it would have been called a "crack" train—the once-a-day special pounding south from Toronto to New York City. The railway company, with a certain poetic flourish, has given it a name: the Maple Leaf. These days, however, eleven hours and thirty-two minutes somehow seems less "crack" than it used to. When I boarded the Maple Leaf at Albany the other evening, it was clear that there weren't many of us who still shared that delicate mix of nostalgia, civility, and leisure necessary for train travel in an airport age.

I had, from the outset, half a car to myself. Now that's a disorienting circumstance. I've been wedged into so many coach-class airline seats in this country, and settled for so many aisle seats on British Rail trains, that I've come to think of traveling as a gregarious and demotic sport. Suitcase in hand, I wandered down the empty, darkened coach (they were changing engines, and we boarded in the semi-gloom of emergency lights), tried several locations that were not to my taste, and finally came upon an alcove whose two pairs of seats faced each other. I chose the forward-facing window seat, hoping the lights inside the coach might be subdued enough to let me glimpse the Hudson River.

But the train pulled out, and the lights came up full, and the window was nothing but a gloss of reflections. I had books and papers at my side, yet nothing called out to be read. So I sat and thought. That, after all, is what trains are good for: promising ample time, they are havens for procrastinators, dreamers, and those who have found the link between idleness and insight.

I found myself recalling a similar alcove a few years ago on a train from London to Scotland. I was with my wife (who likes sitting forward rather than backward) and we were rolling through Yorkshire pastureland in broad daylight. I had recently come (through the bizarre logic that sometimes characterizes changes in career) out of an academic life teaching poetry and into journalism; and I recall thinking that, given my newfound occupation, I was in the wrong seat. Looking backward, I saw only what had just gone by. It occurred to me that I should be sitting where my wife was—that journalism, wedded to the workaday world and intent on spotting trends before they crest, should take the seat on the train facing forward. The backward-looking seat—leisured, contemplative, and rooted in an academic turn of mind that ponders the ever-deepening past—belongs to history. To be sure, both journalists and historians do a good deal of rubber-necking over their shoulders. But their natural pose is straight ahead—the journalist keen to identify the speck on the horizon before it hurtles into the present, the historian content to wait until the massive object that once filled the window recedes and takes its place in perspective among the other objects of the landscape.

The metaphor came and went, and I had only time for a tremor of suspicion at its overly neat two-part structure before something—a herd of sheep, perhaps—sparked a comment from my wife and I craned round to see. So it was not until that night along the Hudson that I came back to the analogy. What was it, I thought, that had made me slightly uneasy?

I was thinking this thought when the lights on the Maple Leaf suddenly blacked out. The train rolled on undisturbed, and soon a maintenance man clanked up the aisle and disappeared into the rear of the diesel engine. I looked out the window. There, dimly lit under the cloudy night, was the river, and beyond it the lights of a town on the far shore and the low mountains so beloved of the painters of the Hudson River School.

It was a glorious sight—mysterious, evocative, and altogether gentle. I spent some moments looking straight out the window, nose close to the glass. Then, abruptly, the lights came on again. River, town, mountains, and sky vanished. I was staring, instead, at a reflection of myself.

Startled, I drew back—but not before I saw what had troubled me in the earlier analogy. What it lacked, I saw, was a third element: the sense of the *now*. If journalism looks forward and history backward, who is watching that illusive evanescence we call the present?

With the question came the answer: the poet.

I sat back with the same relief Dr. Watson must have felt when Sherlock Holmes explained a missing link in an unsolved case. The poet, indeed—the one who catches in sharp detail that moment when the future is just sliding into the past—must always sit sideways, face to the glass. He can glance forward (more readily than the historian) or backward (with greater ease than the journalist)— but only at the risk of losing forever the fleeting image of the now.

I pondered that idea, slowly, carefully. And as I did, I began to see why I had been content to leave the haven of the academy for the hurly-burly of journalism. Poetry has always ridden the Midnight Special of the mind, and for centuries the lights inside were dim; and if the poet's own face showed up in the glass, the reflection was not bright enough to obscure the vision of the world beyond. But these days, the lights inside are at full glare; the poet, searching vainly for an outer world, sees only himself. Solipsistic, self-enwrapped, he comes to see poetry less as a charting of the world's play upon the soul than as a mirror for the ego.

Does that mean I disdain poetry? Not at all: I am calling for balance, for an art that sees beyond the self. I long for a poetry that looks through the same window and into the same world that the journalist and the historian see and know. We are all of us, after all, on the same train.

DEPTHS
ON THE
SURFACE

□

Ice. It hung in spikes from the eaves. It gathered in great cobbled chunks in the downspouts. It grew in frosted thickets inside the storm windows, and rattled like broken bottles along the sidewalks, and lay in shattered panes over the places where puddles used to be. In the rural Massachusetts winters of my youth, it was everywhere.

But most of all, it turned an otherwise indifferent pond in the local woods into a hockey rink. Many a Saturday I gathered up my thickest socks, scrounged among mittens and caps for a puck, and took my tape-wrapped stick from the garage where it leaned incongruously among a sum-mer stack of rakes and spades. Then I would set off for the mile-long trudge through the woods, the black skates with toes like baseballs strung over my shoulder.

I was never very good at hockey. Nor were my friends. Frankly, we never had much chance to practice. We spent most of our time shovelling snow off the makeshift rink. After that, we were too tired to play. So we'd sit on the mounds we'd made and talk, our thick sweaters warm from exertion and the wan winter sun.

That, of course, is the problem with New England ice: a lot of the time there's snow. So the skates, exuding an air of hurt rebuke like dogs you have forgotten to feed, hang in a thousand woodsheds and chimney corners for weeks on end, awaiting that rare season when the freeze comes smoothly across a still night and the cold stands snowless for days.

When that happened, of course, we looked to greater things than our two-bit makeshift rink. I had friends who lived in a village north of town near a mile-long pond. They kept close watch on it. When enough below-zero days had passed, and enough fishermen had been seen strolling across its surface, and enough fathers had looked down the fishing-holes and nodded approvingly at the thickness of the ice, the word went around: there would be a party on Saturday night, down by the church where the road swings close to the shore.

And so we would gather in the cracking cold, with the moon hung like a great lemon ice over the trees, so close you wanted to eat it. Someone would build a fire far out from the shore, dragging out tree trunks to circle it. There we would bend into agonizing shapes, tugging our rebellious laces to tightness—until at last we stumbled into motion, spreading ourselves outward from the fire into our own individual worlds while the ice grumbled beneath us. It was entirely exhilarating. And yet it was somehow so wholly commonplace. I remember thinking, even then, how much I delighted in the experience, yet how little I knew why.

I had occasion to think on these things again recently when, as though flung back twenty winters, I found myself once more on skates. The lake—this time in Maine—was frozen under a snowless afternoon. Again we spread out, putting a quarter of a mile between us with a few minute's effort. Again the ice grumbled, and the great ragged cracks gaped harmlessly beneath our blades. And again, by an entirely natural legerdemain, the impassable depth became an easily charted land.

As we skated that day, I began to grasp what it was that for so many years had appealed to me. It was not just that, like the skaters in a Breughel painting or a Currier and Ives print, we were carrying forward a tradition of almost classic purity, one that had changed hardly at all over the years. Nor was it simply that we were conquering the winter, turning to our advantage the dragon that defends New England from those who care only for warmth. It was more. We were, however accidently, exploring the unknown.

For a frozen lake is always, in some ways, unknown. Map it though we might, it will never again be the same. This black patch of ice over here, that rough and rippled section over there—under the different winds of another year, they will not set up that way again. A tract of unaccustomed territory, it is the creation of a particular season. Like the various people on it—the skaters, the few fishermen, the occasional walker with dogs—its various years have common features of islands and shorelines. Yet each year, like a face or a fingerprint, its details are unique.

How does that uniqueness shape itself? Why does it happen that one year the ice is smooth just by the shore and rippled farther out, when the next year reverses the pattern? Why should it be that, far away from any obstacles to bend the wind, a mirror-smooth midlake patch sits right beside a swirled and rippled washboard surface? Why does ice shade so variously from deep black to opaque white?

I'm sure there is a science governing these effects, and that if we knew it we could explain—perhaps even predict—the entire topography of each winter's lake. But the fact is that, as in more things than we care to admit, we don't know the underlying laws.

We need not look upon the baffled rings of Saturn or the undersea mysteries of the Cayman Trench to sense the limits of our comprehension. Even pond ice throws up its constant queries. It reminds us that we are not as profound as we think, that our so-called laws have hardly touched the depth of nature's grain, that we are skating on the still-unfathomed grandeur of the commonplace.

THE
TROUTING
OF AMERICA

□

'Trout-colored," said my wife, looking across at our neighbor's once-white and now newly painted house.

"I kind of like it," I said tentatively.

"It's nice," she agreed. "But it's trout-colored."

The trouble with such phrases is that they stick like burrs in one's consciousness. Since she said it, I've noticed a strange trend in our town. The sparkling white-clapboard look, once so universal here in New England, is losing its authority. Hardly a street remains that hasn't been brushed at least once by off-whites. Nothing violent, you understand. So far, it's just a subtle nuance here and there along the beige-mauve-taupe axis—a saffron-mayonnaise sea-captain's house down the street, a fried-clam-colored cape up near the woods. But the trend is clearly here. To judge by our corner of coastal Maine, in fact, we may be witnessing the trouting of America.

Now, I admit that I'm not the most unbiased commentator on this development. I grew up in a four-square, two-story New England house that, probably from its building in the 1850s, had been painted white. My father duly renewed that legacy every few years, constructing scaffolding around the entire place and lathering on white lead paint from a brush I could hardly have lifted.

The paint was described as "self-chalking": over time, an oxide would form on the surface that would wash off, renewing its whiteness with every rain. I recall several incarnations of that scaffolding; I recall that the shutters went from forest green to black; but I never recall even a whisper of discussion about the color of the house itself. It was white, and white it would remain.

So whence this creeping troutism of today? It could, of course, be a mere fad, a testament to the spirit of the times. Colors are that way. Each age, it seems, has its prevalent hue. Back in the 1950s, I recall, the toniest bathrooms sported purple and black ceramic tiles. A bit later came the salmon-and-gray Nash Ramblers. Then there was the madras jacket, followed by the loden green coat. More recently, teal blue has had its day. So why not trout?

The trouble is, of course, that coats and cars and bathroom tiles are, to a certain extent, expendable items. They wear out, and you replace them. Houses are more durable. And while each repainting-time opens worlds of possibilities for changing the tint, I suspect most folks are like my father and stick with what they've got. Unless, as I say, a trend sweeps over the community and everybody starts playing musical colors.

Sociologists, noting this trend, no doubt see deep forces at work in the American psyche, of which trout-color is but a portent. They probably link it, in ways I couldn't possibly trace, to two-worker incomes, or the impact of color television, or Europe in 1992, or some such thing. I prefer a simpler hypothesis, which is that we are not so much embracing trout as fleeing from white.

It's not that white is frightening—although, given Herman Melville's chapter in *Moby Dick* on why the whiteness of the whale inspired such dread among the crew, that would be a decent hypothesis. It's just that white is . . . well, so resolutely *white!* A freshly painted white house is so determined in its purity, so relentless in its absolutism. It isn't on its way to being something else, nor does it fall between other hues. It hasn't been created by compromise; it was never blended from a fusion of opposites. It stands at the furthest extreme of the color scale: below it ranges the endless variety of existence, but beyond it there is no place to go. It simply *is*.

In a world of relative achievements and fudged evasions, that's an unsettling thought. Nothing like a gleaming white house, after all, to remind us of our own vulnerabilities, our off-white arguments, our slightly trout-colored ethics. Nothing like the stark clarity of our simpler past to highlight the muddle of our complex present. Nothing like the absolute to rebuke our faith in the relative.

So how do we respond? Time was we would have adjusted our lives to fit our surroundings. Now we repaint our environments to match our consciences. No telling where it will stop, either. In my darker moments, I have visions of New England picture postcards with hot-pink church spires beside paisley parsonages.

Pride, you say? The conceit of a society that wants to remake the world in its own image? Could be. As I say, I'm not one to judge. We live in a gray-shingled house.

WORKING
THE
UNDERBRUSH

☐

I've never been much interested in clothes—as my wife, with a sigh, can attest. I don't say that in bragging. It's just that, unless I make a special effort to look, I never really *notice* them. I couldn't possibly tell you, even after spending an evening with friends, what they were wearing. So you'll understand that what happened the other day—a gray, chill morning that brought the first breath of winter to our tiny Maine village—was, to say the least, unusual.

I had made a date that morning to have the snow tires put on at the local garage—a grease-soaked, joyously untidy sort of place that sells everything from diesel fuel and brake shoes to dish soap and hamburgers. Since I hoped they could correct a few other quirks as well, I left the car and set off for the three-mile walk home.

The first half-mile, along the shoulder of the state highway under bare roadside maples, was uneventful. I passed several dozen houses and the typical landmarks of a rural community: the volunteer fire department housing fire-trucks in the winter and, on summer weekends, chicken suppers; the white-clapboarded one-room post office, sporting window-boxes and a large clock-faced thermometer; the green-shingled well-house on the grassy triangle near the general store; and the store itself. A plastic trailer-sign, parked on a nearby lawn, announced that the storekeepers had their fingers on the town's pulse. "FREE COFFEE," it said, "WINTERIZING NEEDS—SALAMI ITAL 99." Translated literally, it meant that the store sold hot drinks, weatherstripping, and submarine sandwiches. Figuratively, it suggested that here, among the corn flakes and canned peas, could be found conviviality, light hardware, and an inexpensive lunch.

Needing none of the above, I turned up past the school—a low, newish building punctuated with many windows. In its white-simplicity, it looked like what the post office might want to be when it grew up. The near end housed the town offices. Out of the far end, as I walked past, gushed a gaggle of third-graders and a single adult bundled against the cold. Beyond the school lay a lot belonging to the highway department—a giant's sandbox, with a low mountain of gravel and a bright-yellow front-end loader for filling the plow trucks when the snows came and the roads needed sanding.

And there you have it: the intricate network of rural institutions that sociologists ponder, novelists celebrate, and legislators tax. There is what we call a village. But what keeps it running? What do these people do all day? Why does it exist?

I thought about that as the noise of the schoolchildren faded and the road wound into the woods. Ahead I could hear a chain saw. As I topped the rise, I came upon a bright orange truck parked on the shoulder: a tree crew, clearing limbs away from the overhead wires with what is known (even in New England, where hardly anyone harvests cherries) as a cherry-picker. But what gave me pause—stopped me cold for a moment, in fact—was the man who suddenly appeared from behind the truck. He was about my height. Like me, he was clean-shaven. And although he wore a yellow hard hat and I a leather cap, we were in every other way dressed identically: low brown boots, faded jeans, blue work-shirt, navy-blue parka vest, and black gloves.

The world is full of mirrors. We see ourselves reflected in a thousand polished surfaces, each with its own lucidities and distortions. But only rarely, in either fiction or life, do we come upon the living mirror that drives us deep within ourselves to ask not only "Who's that?" and "Who am I?" but "Why are we so alike?"

By the time I had reached the truck, he had climbed in and started it up without so much as a nod. But his image stayed with me as I walked, and with it a larger question. Why was I not the one with the saw, and he the one walking home to an afternoon of reading and writing before the fire?

I tried on a standard, ready-to-wear answer: that he and his fellow maintenance men make it possible for me to do my work more easily. But that answer tried to rank my work above his; it didn't fit. Better, I thought, to turn it inside out: that I exist so that *he* can get on with *his* job, supported in some small way by the money I spend in the town. But that sounded too patronizing—as though, from an avuncular height, I sat showering the village with the largess it needed to keep running.

Behind me, I heard his saw start up. The sound pursued me for perhaps half a mile—for as long as it took, in any case, to puzzle out an answer that, once seen, caused me to stop once again in sheer exhilaration. It's not, I suddenly realized, that he works for me, nor that I work for him. We're both in service to a far larger idea. It's an idea that makes villages (and, therefore, towns and cities and states and nations) work. It's an idea that knits together mechanic and postmaster, teacher and grocer, tax collector and snowplow driver—an idea compounded out of the dignity of labor and the joy of exercising a well-learned skill. It's an idea that depends on the use of widely different means to serve a unified end. It's an idea that requires us to wear our differences as though they were similarities—and to recognize that only out of a respect for diversity is real unity built. The idea is community.

Why I glanced upward just then, I don't know. But my eye caught a nearby telephone pole and its tracery of wires—filled, I knew, with messages. That's it, I thought: the common ground between my look-alike and me. Neither of us knows what all those messages contain. We don't need to. Our role (not plural: the jobs had fused, for me, into a single entity) is simply to trim away whatever threatens those wires. Our job is to keep the communication among people flowing—keep the circuits undamaged, keep the channels of the mind free and active. He worked in the roadside trees. I worked in the verbal underbrush. But season upon season, limb by limb and verb by verb, message-maker and message-defender, we worked alongside each other. Of such shearsmanship, I thought, are villages made.

THE
RACCOON
SHRUGGED

☐

The other day I had a staring match with a raccoon. Or at least that's what *I* thought. He probably thought he was invisible—gazing out through his black mask from the dense hazel bushes along the shore, motionless before the green and alien presence of my canoe.

A moment before, I had come around the point into the marshy shallows. Through the wisps of early-morning mist that rose from the lily pads, I had noticed a movement in the bushes. But there was no hint of wind in the Maine sky. The water lay smooth and pearly, like the inside of a mussel shell. So I let the canoe drift and peered at the bushes, trying to puzzle out the cause of the sudden tuggings and snappings among the leaves. Now and then a paw emerged. Here and there, past gaps in the natural hedge, a banded tail flitted past. At last, as though assembled into a whole by a force beyond us both, the entire animal appeared near a piece of drift-wood. Thirty yards away, my canoe creaked gently against some reeds. We both froze—I with the paddle across the gunwales, he with forefoot on the log.

One can pass a lot of time watching animals. It's an old and honorable tradition, especially in a country conceived as a frontier and dedicated to the proposition that self-sufficiency rewards those who understand the ways of the wild. But before long, the mind wants more than just a stare. If you're an Audubon, I suppose, you begin to focus on visual detail. If you're a Darwin, you think about phylum and class. If you're a Thoreau, you reflect on the way nature holds an unflattering mirror up to humanity. But what if you're just a journalist on holiday? Raccoons rarely make headlines. And even a solid feature story on the *Procyon lotor,* small cousin of the black bear, would want to dwell on its relationship with people— overturned garbage cans, midnight raids on the compost heap, and that sort of thing. Not much newsworthy in a backwoods stare—at least, not as the world counts newsworthiness.

The canoe, still drifting slightly, swung in a dead-slow arc. I had to move my head gradually, owl-fashion, to keep him in view. The longer I sat there, the more I wondered what this encounter meant. In a sense, of course, he was just what I wanted: He was my reward for fumbling out of bed before dawn and paddling through what felt like gelid air. I, however, was distinctly not what he expected—an interruption of his otherwise leisurely forage along a hidden stretch of bog. What gave me the right, then, to satisfy my curiosity at the expense of his breakfast? What could I learn from him *in person* (if the phrase may be stretched to cover coons) that I couldn't have learned more quickly, and certainly more warmly, by reading about him beside the fire back at the cabin?

The canoe, by now, had stopped moving. I began to glimpse, in the black mask of that patient face, what troubled me. His isolation, and my desire to share it, was squarely at odds with journalism. For journalism wants in so many ways to barge in upon that privacy, hale it into public for all the world to see, roll about like hard candy on the gossip's tongue. On one hand, the black mask of the uninvaded wilderness; on the other, the instrusive nose of reportage.

Had it not been for what happened next, I might have left the matter at that—bathing myself in the mixed light of a wilderness morning shaded with a slight occupational shame. But the raccoon suddenly turned away—I'm sure I only imagined that he shrugged— and took up his bushy hunt again. Perhaps he had grown used to my stillness. Or perhaps he had concluded (quite rightly) that a man in a straw hat armed only with paddles at thirty paces was a threat worthy of supreme indifference. But just maybe, knowing that he was being watched, he consciously set out to display raccoonishness (or is it raccoonicity?) in its best possible light— assiduously tipping up logs, hunting under tufts, and fishing through the pickerel-weed with a new-found determination.

So had I really intruded upon a privacy? Or had I merely watched nature at work? Was I uncovering secrets best left undiscovered? Or was I simply bearing witness to the inherent and instructive characteristics of a neighbor? Was this an invasion or an invitation—and, whichever it was, did it make the world a worse or a better place?

One is not usually driven out of swamps by moral wrestlings. But as I paddled home to breakfast, I realized that there, in that indifferent stretch of woods, I had stumbled upon the central dilemma of the reporter's craft. The good reporter—or essayist, or teacher, or artist of any sort—leaves, like that raccoon, no promising stone unturned. Every detail moves toward coherence. Each gesture and word, however haphazard, begins to compose a character—and, through that, a world. All is grist for the mill.

But with curiosity must come also discretion—the sensitivity that knows when insight is distorted into mere gossip, where to draw the line between genuine public discourse and legitimately private intimacies. To maintain the highest regard for the confidential, and the lowest tolerance for the cover-up; to write so that the reader can not only *know* but *understand;* to do it all without being manipulated by one's subjects or duped by one's own excitement—there are days, I thought as I beached the canoe at the cabin, that it must be easier to be a raccoon. What they find, after all, they simply eat—whether or not anyone is watching.

SQUIRREL
BANANAS

☐

As I recall, they were called Squirrel Bananas. They came in yellow and brown waxed-paper wrappings (that was before cellophane was much in fashion) and were shaped like little logs. I think they were at the luxury end of the penny candy spectrum: the wrappers were folded over neatly like Christmas gifts, not merely twisted off like salt water taffy papers. Inside was a sticky brown confection with yellow swirls in it. I never could figure out what it tasted of. I only knew that, along with ham on Sundays and pine-cone fights in the backyard at dusk, they were among the best things in the world.

In those days, the beacons of our school-day afternoons were the small-town candy stores. The one that drew us most frequently was located in a block of brick buildings along Main Street on the route we took home. Sometimes we went uptown instead to the newsdealer or the drug stores. But most of the time we ended up there in Randy's store—a wave of wriggling, jostling boys, slamming open the screen door and surging up against the varnished wood counter.

Randy himself was a jovial fellow. His wife, in the Yankee tradition, was a bit tart: she had a couple of pairs of children herself, and seeing us boil through the door probably soured her even more. But both of them seemed willing enough to spend a great deal of time selling us a nickel's-worth of licorice or a fistful of bubble gum. They would stand aside while we stared at the jars and pondered. And such jars they were! There were gumdrops and caramels, chocolate kisses in foil and hard candies in garish yellows and purples. There were mints and taffies, bonbons and nonpareils, and the polished gleam of fat jelly beans. At Randy's you could even get what we called "hoo-haa balls"—large red spheres, hard as marbles, built up in layers alternating between a pleasant sweetness and a red-hot clovey tang. All you could do to cool the raging tongue as the layers changed was open your mouth wide and breathe "hoo-haa."

But Randy never had Squirrel Bananas—not even when he opened his second store a mile down the street. That was out beyond our house, so we never passed it except on our Saturday expeditions to the river. Even then, we never stopped in. Because just before Randy's other store, we came to Landry's.

Landry's store was more countrified: it stood by itself, a frame building fronting the road with a gravel turnout and a wide wooden porch. But inside was the same counter, the same painted tin ceiling, the same worn wood floor, the same shelves of Duz and Babbo and Postum and Ovaltine. And the same ranks of jars behind the counter. With one difference. One of them held all the Squirrel Bananas you could imagine.

I suppose, now that I think of it, that the Squirrel Bananas were merely a fringe benefit of our trips. I suspect that the real reason for setting out on those Saturday morning jaunts—past the field where the power lines crossed town, past the house of the man who worked nights and whose wife shushed us smartly when we made too much noise, past the Scarboroughs' damply affectionate Saint Bernard, past the black iron fence in front of the spooky brick mansion—I suspect the real reason was to get to the Fort River and its grassy banks. But one can't be sure: had it not been for Landry and his Squirrel Bananas, would we have gone so often?

I don't know. I only know that in those days we stood—though we never knew it—at the edge of an era. We were in the twilight of unwrapped candies: overtaking us, marching in hygienic precision, would come the Age of the Wrapper. Had we but peeped over the horizon, we would have foreseen ranks of candy bars where the jars once stood. We would have seen jelly beans in tight little bags. We would even have seen hoo-haa balls politely packaged in cellophane.

Now I don't mean to quibble over which candies were gooey enough to require wrappers and which had them only for show. Nor do I want to get sidetracked into questions of litter—how many trees it takes to make the paper or barrels of oil to make the plastic that goes into the wrappers we pluck from our hedges or sweep from our streets. That's a subject for other days, other hands. No, the point here is a broader one. It is that we led, in those days, a kind of unwrapped life. I knew boys, to be sure, whose Saturdays were as deftly packaged as a Squirrel Banana: piano lesson, tennis lesson, haircut, lawn mowing, and so on. Ours were more open: we set out on our own, exploring the sidestreets, tramping through the woods, wading under the bridge. And always, come Saturday, there were more things to do than you could imagine: hours as richly varied as those widemouthed jars, and life, like a jovial shopkeeper, standing by while we made up our minds.

DIGGING
TO CHINA

☐

In those days I was not very tall, and the red-shanked spade, with its square-edged blade and short oak handle, was the only shovel I could manage. My father had others in the shed—long-handled and pointed like the prows of ships, or flat and broad for scooping up grain and snow. We even had a post-hole digger, a massive nutcracker that pinched fingers and strained elbows as it dug its little round holes.

But the spade was best. You planted it firmly in the turf and leaped on it with both sneakered feet. In it went, shearing a clean thin line. Three more like it in a square, and you could lift out a clod of turf by its hair. And there beneath was the New England earth, calling us to dig as far as we dared. Even, we thought, to China.

In those days, the field across the street grew grass in waves, cresting and breaking under the summer wind. It was there that our plans to reach China took shape. We even punched a few test holes here and there—until the day our third-grade teacher got to talking about volcanoes and magma and the red-hot center of the world. After that our plans changed. We never admitted that we had given up the China venture, but we settled for digging forts and caves instead.

Long before we got there the field had been purchased by the electric company, which burned it over each year and kept it as a right of way for its high-tension lines. Years before that, it must have been an orchard: under one of the pylons stood three aging apple trees, which, despite their blossoming promise each spring, produced but a scanty crop of misshapened and sour fruit in the fall.

Then, during the war, the field had been laid out into victory gardens. I can still remember, as a tot, hearing the chink of hoes and the soft babble of voices as neighboring families tended their vegetables in the still summer evenings. Some years later, when the war was gone and the grass had again taken victory over the gardens, I dug up a freshly grown carrot—part of a stock still seeding itself, no doubt, from those family plots. It too was hard and gnarled, and warm from the sun. I wiped it clean on my sleeve, and bit into it. It was, and remains to this day, the sweetest carrot I have ever tasted.

But it was up in the corner where the Central Vermont railroad tracks crossed Whitney Street that we did our serious digging. It was here that we built our fort against the enemies—who, in the form of several fourth-graders living across the field, were sure to be plotting deep and mischievous intrigue against our defenses.

First we dug a shoulder-deep pit the size of a child's bed. Then we overlaid our hole with stout beams, smaller

sticks, and a layer of cut grasses. We left a small hole in one corner where the ladder went down. And so we crouched in its coziness, fancying ourselves protected from our foes by the skillful camouflage of our thatch. In fact, they probably never bothered to look for us— although one day some weeks later, long after we had wearied of hiding there waiting for Something Sudden to happen, we returned to find the beams staved in and the thatch scattered.

Not that it mattered. By then we had discovered that the hill in the woods behind our house, though dirt on the surface, was actually sand—pure orange-white sand, without rocks or roots, and packed so hard that the spade could carve it into straight-sided, tough-ceilinged tunnels and caves. In the months that followed it became a regular rabbit warren of holes and channels—while the spade, to my father's occasional annoyance, spent weeks away from its home in the shed.

But the fall rains came, and school set in, and the next year, as I recall, we got into hammers and nails and building lumber huts. The holes crumbled and the tunnels collapsed; and it wasn't long before there was no sign left of a boy's unreasoned fascination with digging in the earth.

What were we after, anyway? I've asked myself that many times since, when some householder's task again puts me behind a shovel to plant a shrub or set a fence post. Why, in those days, did the simple act of digging produce such unreasoned delight, such a sense of purpose and passion and power?

Part of it, I suppose, has to do with the hunger to construct, to make out of the randomness of soil or sand a structured whole—as a toddler, faced with a pile of blocks, begins at once to stack and order them around him. Part of it, too, must have to do with the drive to use tools. For in nothing do grown-ups seem to have more power and authority than in their capacity to wield tools deftly—driving nails straight, slicing carrots into even disks, and doing so simply the thousand things which to a child seem hopelessly difficult. Maybe a shovel, as a most straightforward tool, promises quickest victory over the challenges of a child's life.

But beneath that, I think, lies an even greater longing: the simple, central thirst for depth. We adults know about that—know it not only as tool-users skilled in the arts of cutting and boring, but as word-crafters probing our surroundings with words. To grow up is to understand how much depth matters, how much life depends on slicing the spade of language through the red-hot centers of experience and into the rich chinoiserie of the world's far shore.

I know some people fear such delving. I might, too, were it not for the memory of the burrowed coziness, the strength of the walls, the sense of containment and protection. There was nothing dark or murky about those spaces. Like well-dug lives, they seemed to grow brighter and lighter the ar her we went. They were illuminations— victories of structure, triumphs of tool—using, small prefigurings of the days when the pen, replacing the spade, would steer through ever-brightening depths to other Chinas.

EVERY INCH
A RAFT

□

Gazebo, belvedere, pagoda—the names are as varied as the parts of the world from which they came. Ours, true to the New England soil on which it stood, was simply called "the summerhouse." It was nothing but a rough-shingled roof, four bark-covered cedar corner-posts, and a plank floor. It stood on a slight rise, afloat on a broad lawn flowing down through flower gardens and lapping at the foundation-stones of our Victorian house. In its shabbiness and structured informality, it seems in memory like something out of a nineteenth-century English landscape painting.

Rural Massachusetts, however, was not so quaint: the weather had some most un-English quirks. Over the years, the snows had weighed heavily on the roof, and the ice had wedged apart the planks. In the spring the mosquitoes drove out any seekers of evening leisure; by the heat of August, the lush grape vines growing up the posts made it a dark and breezeless chamber. It was in the last stages of collapse when my father finally gave it his full attention. A few weeks later he was finished: the summerhouse, honoring a change of taste that would send the backyard gazebo the way of the buggy whip, had become a garage for our camping trailer.

For some years the discarded cedar cornerposts lay in a heap at the edge of the woods. "Might come in handy," my father and I would observe as, year by year, I grew through the age of insouciance and toward adolescence. And one early summer, when the grapes were still green among their hand-shaped leaves and somebody had given me a copy of *Huckleberry Finn,* the purpose of those posts suddenly became clear. With several friends and a crateful of tools, we transformed them into a raft.

And such a raft! We laid on the lawn the cedar posts side by side to form a rectangle. We decked it over with planks. At the bow, a rope; at the stern, a rudder. Over it all, from a pole planted amidships, flew a white flag. It was, to all appearances, the perfect raft for a summer bunch of Tom Sawyers.

But it was more than a mere toy. Deep in the woods of the bird sanctuary a half-mile away was the pond. Somehow, with brute determination rushing in where foresight feared to tread, we jimmied the lumber contraption off the lawn and onto my red wagon. Tottering over the sidewalks, stumbling through the underbrush, we wrenched and panted our way to the shore and slid the raft into the water. Triumphantly, it floated. Without another thought we clambered aboard, our paper sacks of lunch in hand. And gently and steadily, impelled by natural laws indifferent to the astonishment of four small boys, it sank—first to our ankles, then to our knees, and finally to our waists.

We scrambled back to shore and unloaded, but to no avail: those cedar posts, which had held up so much snow for so many winters, were simply too small. In the end, surrendering our visions of luncheon on the sunny deck, we settled for a one-man crew—our smallest member, clutching the flagpole in shin-deep water as the raft drifted along the shore.

I suppose, looking back, you could call it a fruitful failure. Like many such failures, it has parceled out its lessons patiently over the years. The first we learned almost instantly: Trudging home with the wagon, we left the raft half-grounded on the weedy shore, thereby learning (as the economists say) not to throw good money after bad. Other lessons came during bright winter mornings at school: Archimedes and his bathtub, the concept of specific gravity, and the incompressibility of fluids all added their explanations to our failure.

But in the end it was not through science but through my early efforts at writing that, quite by fluke, I came to terms with my raft experience. I had done with the raft what I suppose all writers do now and then: written a nicely designed and carefully crafted piece that said all the wrong things. It, too, was made (as so much writing is) of left-over ideas from an earlier structure—made, as it were, of old posts and beams found at the edge of one's verbal woods. It had a bow and a stern and a rhetorical flourish amidships. It cost a long day's labor to produce and a heavy trudge to deliver. And it, too, sank, inexorably and without apology, into the depths of unpublishability.

Literary critics, when they discuss this sort of thing, talk of form versus content. I've always distrusted that distinction—believing, with the poet William Butler Yeats, that you cannot tell the dancer from the dance. Yet there it was: high-gloss prose draped over insubstantial argument.

And there we once were, four lads in a green-grape summer, holding so surely to our sense of form that we never gave a thought to content. It was, as I say, an absolutely lovely structure, every inch a raft. And it sank.

TRASH
AND THE
MAN

☐

I grew up not far from a dump.

My wife, I'm sure, finds that deeply significant. She has spent years weaning me of careless messiness—teaching me to put the Scotch tape back into the second drawer, not to leave the grass clippers on the front step, and not, as she says, to "play ducky" when I wash my face, soaking everything within splash-range of the bathroom sink.

I confess to the benefit of her tutelage. Any unbiased observer, I'm sure, will find me a neater man than I was. Which is why, before I cede to neatness whatever tolerance for disorder I once had, I want to account for the place that dump played in my formative years.

It was no ordinary dump. It was nothing but a steep incline between an old clapboard house and the railroad track that bisected our rural New England town. But the Yankee folk who once lived there, no doubt mixing an esthetic distaste for the iron leviathans in their backyard with a practical out-of-sight-out-of-mind attitude, pitched over the slope whatever had outlived its usefulness. So by the time I came along, a ten-year-old with a packrat instinct and a taste for gadgetry, it was a trove of bed-springs, rusted-out oil drums, shattered bottles, and wash-ing-machine lids—a whole Sears catalog of wood, metal, glass, and rubber shapes. "I don't know—it might come in handy," I would invariably reply when my mother, stumbling over some frightfully heavy shaft of rusted steel by the back steps, asked me questions beginning, "Why on earth . . . ?"

A lot of it, I had to admit, really was junk. But one day, sorting among the rubble under the spindly trees that had shot through the rubbish, I found a prize which probably changed my life. It was a baby-carriage frame, a spring-like contraption in the form of several tipped-over G-clefs. It bore two steel axles and—most astonishingly— four excellent rubber-tired and wooden-spoked wheels.

I carted it home in triumph. For years we had used the steep street leading up to the tracks as a racecourse, careening down it on red wooden wagons. But here, I saw, was the very stuff from which to build a proper racing-cart. Our driveway became a litter of planks, saws, nails, and rope. At last, in a flurry of exaltation, I dragged the finished product to the hill-top, grabbed the steering ropes, and let fly.

Now, no doubt a bright twelve-year-old might have suspected a fundamental weakness that, as I flew gleefully down the hill, had not yet occurred to me. It was not, I assure you, that I forgot a brake. That was kid stuff: you used your heels.

No, what defeated me was centrifugal force. At the bottom of the hill I had to turn rather sharply into the driveway. And the weak, delicately-milled wheels, made to carry nothing more than a baby at two miles an hour, simply couldn't take the strain of turning. They quite literally exploded. I recall innumerable spokes flying about my head like bowling pins, the cart smashing down heavily onto its hubs, and a small, shocked boy clutching the steering-rope—while a single rubber-tired rim, somehow still upright, bounced merrily on down the street.

In the following months, my father must have taken pity on me. I scavenged up some wire-spoked wheels, and he offered to help me build a Real Racing Car. And what a car it was: a long oak-framed affair that would have made Bugatti's mouth water! It had a curved cowling of bent plywood, a seatback cut from a barrel, a sophisticated hand-and-foot brake system (Mother was by this time tired of finding my loafers with the heels worn off at steep and unusual angles), and a real steering wheel. We painted it royal blue, put a large silver "11" (my age) on the side, and took Whitney Street by storm.

The cart is long gone. The dump by now must be wholly overgrown. But the feel of those days remains. I'm aware that my creation of racing carts started as a random encounter between a curious mind and the thrown-out leavings of someone else's life—the happy conjunction of a need I didn't know I had with an object nobody thought was useful. But something clicked somewhere: looking at one thing, I saw another.

And that, as somebody once said, is the basis of metaphor. I no longer raid dumps and bring home barrel staves. I raid conversations and books, carting off images, concepts, details, facts, statistics—whatever the language happens to toss up. And again and again they come in handy: scraps of this, lying beside pieces of that, fuse in the process we so loosely call "inspiration." The mind seizes on a connection, ideas flow, the typewriter starts.

The French literary critics have a word for it: *bricolage*. A *bricoleur* is one who, finding the scraps tossed aside by mere logic, fashions literary constructions out of what happens to be lying about.

Bricolage, certainly, accounts for a lot of modern poetry—the almost random play of a mind seeing relations among things which most of us would leave separate. It is the basic thrust behind junk sculpture, musical improvisation, and, I suspect, some of the world's best dinnertable conversation and finest speeches. I can't help thinking that even a Shakespeare or a Virgil knitted into their writing images which just happened to be at hand— the result of a book read yesterday, a chance remark the day before. They must have known the value of "junk." Perhaps they would have been able to tell us—in an age increasingly awash with litter—that one shouldn't flee from junk so much as transform it.

Junka, as Virgil would never have said, *virumque cano:* I sing of trash and the man.

A CELLAR
TO CALL
ONE'S OWN

☐

N ew England, to the great comfort of those of us who delight in our own and others' childhoods, is a place of basements.

I realize this may sound terribly quaint to those Sunbelt readers whose houses need nothing more than thin slabs of concrete beneath them. I will grant them their sunshine, and their relative ease of building, and even their indifference to having the crawl space flooded. I lived happily among them for years. But here in New England we have what's called a frost line, below which you must dig your foundation—and lay your water mains—unless you want the most appalling heaves and bucklings of pipes and walls when winter comes. Hence the basement. And hence one of the inestimable delights of childhood: a cellar to call one's own.

I was two when we moved into the hundred-year-old Massachusetts basement (with, of course, a house attached) that I would come to think of as home. No doubt I was prevented, by a particularly steep set of stairs and an alert mother, from exploring it right away. My earliest memories of it include lumps of coal left over from the pre-oil days, a firewood pile, and my father's shop, and some dim and spooky regions stretched out under the kitchen ell. As I think back on it, it was everything a boy's basement should be: walled in great chunks of stone, floored in cement, and giving onto the side yard through sloping bulkhead doors covering wide granite steps. Yet for all its unshakable stability, it had a marvelous fluidity, an unlimited potential for the imagination. Because it was undeveloped, it was infinitely flexible; being a kind of nothing, it could become, in a boy's mind, everything.

One year, I recall, it was submarines. At that time my brother was a ham radio buff, and his corner of the basement was a mine of wires, knobs, and old radio chassis stacked in a halfway discarded state. We pillaged that pile (with his belated and grudging permission, I recall) and lugged off what, in our eyes, were radar scanners, sonar bleepers, and vastly sophisticated pieces of torpedo launching equipment. Our hull, on which we mounted this gear, was a series of large cartons, with judicious amounts of garden hose and rope linking its various chambers. It was there, in that basement, that we toured the Atlantic, fought off evil, and liberated Europe.

Then there was the night when we discovered the delights of hide-and-seek with the lights off. Why my mother permitted a rabble of pre-teen-age boys to howl through her cellar late into the evening I have never understood. Perhaps she didn't know. Or perhaps, seeing our disorder contained by granite rather than by finer textures upstairs, she knew more than we thought. She may have known that there wasn't a boy around whose imagination could outrun the capacity of that cellar to give it play.

In later years, it took on different looks. For a while it was chemistry sets in one corner and radios in another. Then it was a long and lingering apprenticeship at my father's woodworking tools. Finally we walled off one corner into a kind of music room, complete with couches, dim lights, piano, and what in those days was called a hi-fi. I even pressed the bulkhead stairway into unusual service once when, during college, my crumbling Jaguar needed new main bearings. We timbered up two sloping tracks above the stairs, drove the car up onto them, and crouched on the steps beneath to pull off the oil pan.

And through it all, the basement remained much the same. I suppose, in many ways, we shifted faster than it did—like a good book which, though different each time you read it, changes you more than you change it. Living in cellars, in fact, is a little like reading: It fosters an imagination that all the skillfully contrived store-bought playhouses, or all the visually dazzling movies and television shows, can never match.

For basements are largely mental constructs. I suppose we grow up and out of them only as we find other kinds of expansiveness, other undefined sweeps of space and opportunity. Beneath this sort of expansiveness—wherever it rises to excellence—I suspect there is always a basement. The superstructure rises. The cellar remains, a deep foundation of the imagination in an age too used to slabs.

NEXT DOOR
A QUIET
BALM

☐

I was about six years old when she first swam into my
ken. Her square yellow house sat just uphill from ours
through a border of pines. On summer evenings, as I lay
in my bedroom with the sun still bright in the sky, I could
hear her through the screen, talking now and then to her
husband in a voice high and angular and yet somehow
pleasant. She was a short, ample woman of flowered
dresses, with a storybook kitchen full of pie smells. It had
a high-legged white enameled stove—the sort a small boy
could readily have crawled under—and a pantry with
cupboards rising to unreachable and mysterious heights.
Her name was Mabel Jones.

I used to visit that pantry almost weekly, bringing eggs
from a farmer who was a friend of my parents. I would
arrive with the gray egg-carton held gingerly in both
hands and the week's price lodged precariously in my
easily distracted memory. When both had been properly
delivered, she would shuffle into the pantry, take a small

cloth purse from a drawer, and count out some coins. Most of the time they included pennies. Sometimes she added a cookie. We rarely talked.

Her husband's name was Floyd, and he was a mailman. He spent his days delivering other people's words, and he evidently felt that that was sufficient involvement with the language for any man. As near as I could tell, he hardly ever spoke; and in my pine-cone throwing days, such taciturnity seemed both majestic and frightening. I would see him out mowing his lawn (which, as a practiced walker, he did with meticulous patience), or painting his house, or sitting in the wooden rocker on his front porch. I once went with my father to borrow his ladder, and he led us, amid gruff assertions about the weather, into the must and dimness of his garage. I remember marveling that, unlike the dull neatness of our cemented garage, his was floored in hardpacked earth. He had no car.

We, of course, did; and as we drove about we would see him, now and then, delivering mail. His route lay far across our spread-out college town, leaving him a three-mile walk back home. Meanwhile some stranger, living who knows where, delivered our mail. I once asked why they couldn't simply swap routes. Nobody seemed able to give me an answer, so I concluded that it didn't much matter. But I never felt quite the same about the post office after this realization about Mr. Jones.

The most delightful thing about their household, however, was the dog. He was a graying German shepherd, slow and placid, with the incongruous name of Zip. I remember noticing, when alphabetizing attacked me in third grade, that the three neighborhood dogs all had names starting in Z. Moreover, they rose alphabetically from Zach (in the house down the street from ours) through Zeke (our mongrel) and on to Zip. As I think back on it, the progression was partly biblical: the boxer was no doubt named after Zacharias, and our hound owed his name to Ezekiel. Zip, I suspect, was simply himself, with no thought for Zippor or Zipporah.

However his name arose, he was as much a creature of habit as his master. Mornings, as Mr. Jones left in his blue-gray uniform, Zip left for his own tour. He would trot across our front yard and turn up Whitney Street, to reappear twenty minutes later coming down the hill on the other side of his own house. He, too, had his appointed rounds; and though I would not swear that neither rain nor sleet nor snow ever kept him snuggled in that sweet-smelling kitchen, I recall that the neighbors behind us used to claim they could set their clocks by him.

You could set all kinds of clocks, literally and figuratively, by the Joneses. As I see them now through the later-blooming branches of a literary life, they seem almost characters out of fiction—the quintessential neighbors, the archetypal old folks, the familiar spirits of the early 1950s. But were they really closet intellectuals? I don't think so. Children, after all, are the ones who see the undersides of things—who notice the tags on the bottoms of tables and the places the painter missed. So, too, they look up at adults from underneath, and color them in primary hues. And while they may not comprehend complexity, they sense it.

No, I suspect there really was something entirely uncomplicated about the Joneses. They were genuinely sober. In a town full of academic probings, they were honestly simple. And now, in an age awash with the notion that only the articulate are significant, they bob gently upon the surface—just Floyd and Mabel, two buoys marking a quiet channel.

KINDLING
WET
WOOD

□

I'm not sure what it was that used to wake me up. It may
have been the early-morning sunlight, dappling the slanting tent-side with patterns of moving leaves. Or it might
have been the crackle of kindling behind the iron door of
the camp stove, mingling with my father's half-melodic
whistling. Or maybe it was the resinous scent of the red-
cedar smoke that drifted through the mosquito netting to
blend with the tarry odor of warming canvas. Perhaps
they all conspired together, calling a drowsy seven-year-
old to make one last turn on his air mattress, fling back
the dampish flannel sheet, and sit up to stare dumbly out
under the tent-flap.

We had pitched, that summer, at the far point of the
campground, with a view of the lake on one side and
the gurgle of a frog-filled stream on the other. The sites
were spacious, and the Ontario Department of Lands and
Forests had spared no effort to grade them smooth. Each
had a massive picnic table, built of brown-stained logs

and stovebolts that would have stopped a charge of the Mounties. And each had its own cookstove. Fortress-like and blockish, constructed of rounded boulders and rough mortar, it climbed to the height of my chest before leveling off for the two circular stove-lids that covered the firebox. Then it took off again, tapering to a chimney-top well above my head. When my mother wasn't looking, I would hoist myself up on the boulders to peer down the blackened stack.

My father had grown up around cookstoves, so firing it up each morning was as easy as brushing his teeth. Taking the ax, he'd split a short cedar log into inch-thick shakes. Then, bracing a shake against another log with his boot, he'd split it into sticks. If we had some newspaper, he'd crumple it up and put it into the firebox; if not, he'd whittle a handful of cedar shavings to start the blaze. Now and then, when I awoke early, I would watch him from my bed. One morning, thinking to surprise him, I got up before he did, found some wood split from the night before, and laid the fire myself. First I put in the largest log I could find. Then I stacked on some smaller ones. Finally I topped the whole thing off with a wad of paper, jammed tightly under the stove lids. He was genuinely surprised. As he patiently unpacked the firebox and reassembled things right way up, paper on the bottom, he instructed me in the finer points of convection. I think he felt taken aback that one so willing could be so wrong— and a bit guilty that he hadn't explained firebuilding to me earlier. The next day he helped me lay a proper fire.

In the years since then, I've built fires all over the place—in cookstoves, wood furnaces, outdoor incinerators, indoor fireplaces, backyard barbecues, against rock ledges in the woods, and in windy hollows on the dunes. As a child, I seem to recall, I set a neighboring field on fire several times—once by accident and a second time (because the first proved such a great event) only partly so. Later I helped burn down a barn—legally, with the blessing of the local firemen, because it stood where a pond needed digging and would sooner or later have fallen down by itself.

So after all those fires it came as a surprise the other day to find myself in front of a fireplace for a full twenty minutes—alternately blowing, poking, and waiting for the fire to catch. I knew I'd done almost all the right things. But I suspected, too, that the logs were wet and green—not just a rainwater dampness that barely penetrates the grain, but the inner wetness of uncured wood used too soon after cutting. The flames from the kindling surrounded it as they would a rock, died back to a flicker, and fell to coals. The logs just sat there, blackened and unburnt.

What to do? You can't exactly take the wood out, charred and smoking, and put it back in the woodbox. The only recourse is to add dry wood, thrust in more kindling, and hope the mix will work. It is, in some ways, an act of redemption. You find yourself on your knees—gently stacking the tiniest twigs over the smallest of coals, and then, face close to the ashes, blowing firmly (but not too hard) until the flame leaps up. Next you stack on the slightly bigger bits—always careful not to smother the flame nor topple the fragile tent of twigs. At just the right moment—after the flame is in full blaze, but while there's still kindling enough to last a while—you stack on the larger logs. If making a good fire is a skill, redeeming a bad one is an art. Like all artistry, it both taxes the patience and absorbs the intuitions: you have to feel just when to press on and when to let up.

That day, as I waited and watched for the fire to take, I reflected on these things. On one hand, it seemed that my constant, attentive presence was essential to the fire's success. Yet on the other hand I felt I was but an agent in an event far beyond my own making. "Make" a fire? Only the blind language of pride could fashion such a phrase. The fire, like life, makes itself. Then what do we do? We set match against brick, but we're not the cause of the flame. Nor are we the source of fuel—although without us the tree would never meet the grate. We're but mid-wives to a birth, nurses to a growing, witnesses to a strength—chopping, splitting, feeding, tending, reviving the fire in decline, reveling in its robustness, bearing witness to the perpetuation of a glow.

I suppose that's what my father was doing, too—what all parents and educators do. There must have been days when I struck him as pretty wet wood—damp behind the ears, damp inside the head, and generally incombustible. That's when he'd show up with a handful of twigs, blow gently on the coals, and stand back. . . .

DAWN
AND THE
LADY-SLIPPER

□

It was the sort of dawn that made you want to shout. The sun, having messed about in the treetops, now shot flat across the lake. The June breeze, which had peeped and muttered all night among the pines, was busy lip-lapping the waves against the canoe. Even the dog, sitting sideways in the bow as I paddled, trembled with expectation, whining impatiently and jangling his license.

It was, after all, the first morning of a new Maine season; and as usual the drive up from the city the night before had seemed not only a journey into another place but almost into another consciousness. When last we had seen the lake, the ice was just going out. Now, striking out across the open water, we slipped through the narrows into the lee of the point, covered with pine pollen. Coasting close to shore to let the dog jump out, I settled back for the year's first slow and thoughtful paddle among the flora and fauna.

Or at least the flora. The dog bashed and rattled through the underbrush: you could hear him for a hundred yards. So, apparently, could the animals. The only thing on view above songbird size was a duck—which flushed, squawking, before I could discern its markings.

Not that the markings would have helped, I thought uneasily. For all the time I've spent in Maine, I'm not very good at spotting nature's telltales. I know a beaver from a muskrat, and a loon from a Canada goose in good light. But when the conversation shades off into questions of wood ducks and female mallards, I become a mere spectator. I ought to know the differences, just as I ought to know wildflowers. But I don't.

That morning, however, something was different. Maybe it's that the early morning is a time for forgiveness—all that fresh sunlight rinsing away last night's inadequacies. Or maybe it's just that the dog (who by then was standing atop an exposed rock, puffing like a locomotive) left me nothing else to look at but the flora. Whatever the reason, I found myself vowing to pay more attention to the vegetable kingdom—to get to know Maine not only for its exclamatory glimpses of deer and fox but for the stiller voices of the moss and fern.

So I set a course close to the shore and reminded myself to be observant. That much, anyway, I've learned from journalism: that what you see when you're just passing by is nothing compared with what you see when you're consciously watching. So I noticed the catkins on the white birches. I saw last year's leaves still clinging to the oaks, even as this year's squeezed out around them. I saw the white pines and the red pines and the spruce and the firs—and remembered that I did indeed know the differences among them. Maybe, I thought to myself, I know more about Maine than I realize.

Yet it was with a twinge of shame that I recalled something I had blurted out to my wife in the car the night before. "I'm always slightly embarrassed," I had said, "to have to drive around Maine with Massachusetts license plates!" I had meant it, too. We'd done a spot of shopping on the trip, and I'd ordered a pair of trousers. "Where would you like them sent?" asked the sales-woman in a Down East accent. "Boston," I replied, trying not to sigh. Anywhere in the world, it seems, you can say you're from Boston with ringing pride—except in north-ern New England. The slight up-tick of her chin, the hint of a grin around her lips—"I suspected as much," they seemed to say, even as her pen forgivingly took down the address and her jovial "Thank you!" almost hid her conde-scending tone of voice.

Now, in the morning light, my sensitivities seemed unworthy. I grew up in Massachusetts, I reasoned: why should I feel so apologetic? Was I worried about my own credentials, my own license? Did I fear that I, too, was but a tourist?

I had come around a point into the breeze, and had to dig the paddle in hard to keep from being turned around. No, I thought as I made for the next cove, I am *not* a mere tourist. "I am a native in this world"—the words from a Wallace Stevens poem sprang suddenly to mind—"and think in it as a native thinks." A native, yes. To prove it, I feathered the blade, still-paddled noiselessly up to the steep rock ledge, and held the canoe motionless a few inches from the shore.

And suddenly, out of nowhere, came the dog. With a single bound he was down the ledge and into the canoe. We lurched crazily away from the shore, scuffing the bottom on the rocks as we went. "Knock it off!" I yelled, ramming the paddle (as no good canoeist ever does) into the graveled lake-bed for support. The dog looked at me indifferently. "I've had my run," he seemed to say with a drenching shake, "and now I want my breakfast!"

So we turned toward home. As we made our way back along the shore I remembered a verse from the book of Psalms. "I am a stranger in the earth," it reads; "hide not Thy commandments from me."

Stranger? I suppose so, yes. The native, as it were, knows without having learned. The stranger is always in awe of what remains to be known. No, I thought, I am not native to Maine: There's just too much left to learn.

We were approaching the last point. Ahead lay the rough chop of open water. It would be a vigorous paddle home, and I was feeling strangely deflated. Not a Mainer: I could admit that. But am I any more native to Massachusetts? I wondered. And if not, then where *do* I belong?

Taking a last glance at the mossed shore, my eye fell on a lady-slipper. Solitary, pink, and rare, it stood quietly in its niche on the ledge. It needs no license to do that, I thought. Yet in its way it, too, was a stranger—not because it came and went or felt itself out of place, but simply by virtue of a design so strange and wonderful that it might have come from another world.

At that moment, I realized that, like lady-slippers, human beings are at one and the same time both natives and strangers. It was inescapable—a comforting and, at the same time, a stimulating thought.

I would have paused longer, but the wind was plucking at the bow. I remembered that I had seen something about lady-slippers in a tourist book on Maine in the cabin. When I get back, I promised myself, I'll look it up.

CAPACITY
TO
TERMINATE

☐

The other day I read that a congressional staff committee had just completed a six-hundred-page report on
something—a highway interchange, maybe, or an alleged
flaw in the postal service. I don't recall. I do recall that my
thought turned to a basement in Williamsburg, Virginia.
There, beside a replica of a colonial press, the resident
printer hourly explains how to ink the plate, insert the
single sheet, pull on the press lever with enough force to
squeeze the impression into the fibers of the paper, and
remove the finished text for drying—each step done by
hand, and by arm and back as well.

Not far from his cellar is the Capitol, where the General Assembly met. They were, to judge by their record,
reasonable and intelligent men. And they were so, apparently, in spite of a glaring lack of six-hundred-page
reports. In an age less hurly-burly and headlong than
ours, they might have had time to read such things; but,

not having the machinery to print and distribute them, they never bothered to invent them.

Not that knowledge about highways and mails is unimportant. It matters now as it mattered then. The problem lies in our *approach* to these things. There is a lesson in the way in which we address ourselves, through a surfeit of words, to such issues. The lesson is that invention has become the mother of necessity.

Is this mere wit and word-play? Not at all. Having invented a machine which prints, collates, staples, addresses, and mails fat reports with eye-boggling speed, we are compelled, willy-nilly, to discover necessities for its use. Its voracious appetite howls for more copy, more words to print; the machine, ultimately, masters the user. Not physically, of course, for in fact it mightily reduces the strain on arms and backs. The mastery is in ways at once less noticeable and more disturbing. It masters our priorities, causing us to believe in the necessity for first deluging every issue with a torrent of words. We *need,* it seems, to keep saying more and more—a necessity mothered, in large part, by the invention.

This glut is sometimes referred to, with poisonous self-flattery, as "the knowledge explosion." In fact, it is nothing more than a print explosion, and the poison comes from flattering ourselves that *print* equals *knowledge*. The poison is guilt—the guilt we all suffer from knowing that we have not read even a tenth of what we "ought" to have read. Where is the literate man or woman who has not suffered the pangs of self-condemnation at the sight of piles of unread papers, journals, magazines, books? Keeping up, it seems, is impossible. Francis Bacon, they say, was the last man to

146

know everything—which only means that he was the last to keep pace with printing, to be reasonably sure he had read most good things.

That was 350 years ago. By the time of the General Assembly in Virginia there was already too much to read, though even in the eighteenth century a good deal of it was not worth its foolscap. It was left to a nineteenth century Massachusetts poet, however, to grasp the problem and cameo the solution in seven words. The poet was Emily Dickinson. The words are:

> Capacity to Terminate
> Is a Specific Grace.

Our own later age testifies to the aptness of her words. On every side are strewn the relics of those who knew only how to begin. The boarded-up shop, the perennial debt, the soured relationship, the dragged-out committee meeting, the unfinished term paper—getting in seems so much easier than getting out. The capacity to terminate—to bring to a conclusion in proper and timely fashion—is, as she so keenly observed, more "specific" than widespread, not given to masses but demonstrated by individuals. Yet it is a "grace," an ability bestowed freely and open-handedly on those who can comprehend its use. Emily Dickinson's heaven may not have been long on benevolence; but it must have smiled its kindliest on those who, possessed of the soul of brevity, knew how to end.

Even students of poetry, who are learning lots about saying much in few words, fall into the pits of interminability. When I taught college, my students were filled with ideas for papers and reports. Yet they habitually pled the same excuse: "I can't seem to begin." In that assertion, they were (as I tried to say as tactfully as I could) dead wrong. The problem is not beginning but ending. They get so involved hunting for books that they can't stop looking and start reading. Then they can't break off reading to begin thinking. Nor can they be sure when to stop jotting down thoughts and begin composing the text. And, not uncommonly, they get so carried away counting their own pages that they can't end. The cure? "Capacity to terminate."

"But how do you know," comes the anguished cry, "when to stop?" There's no rule. It's a simple process of intuition. Simple, as in knowing when to stop eating or sleeping or exercising—though these things sometimes come hard to us overindulgers. I guess it's just a feeling. The ideas begin to take shape, the words start to coalesce, and suddenly—often long before you're sure you have anything much to say—you know you need to quit everything else and start writing.

So it is with conclusions. There's a world of difference between merely stopping and really concluding. The writers who only know how to stop are the ones who produce six hundred dull pages. They write away from the beginning, never quite knowing how to end it all. The writers who know how to conclude write toward the ending. When they get there, intuition says, "Stop." So they do.